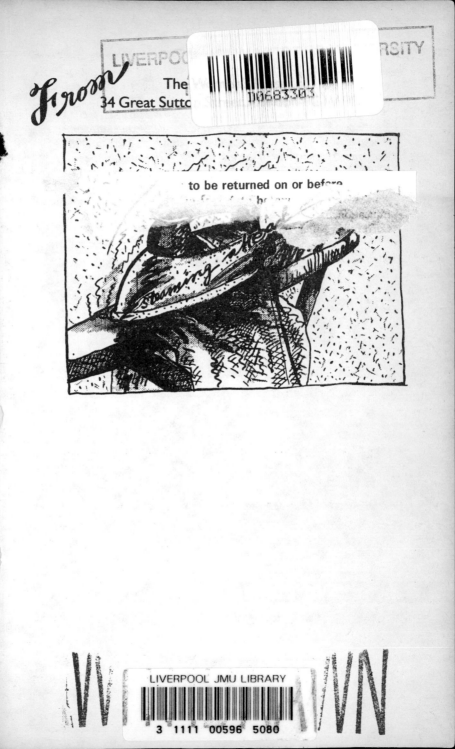

Liz Stanley was born in Portsmouth in 1947. She edited *The Diaries of Hannah Cullwick* (1984, Virago), co-wrote with Sue Wise *Breaking Out: Feminist Consciousness and Feminist Research* (1983, Routledge & Kegan Paul) and *Georgie Porgie: sexual harassment in everyday life* (1987, Pandora), and co-edited *Men and Sex* (1984, Pergamon). A survivor of the gay (men's) movement of the early 1970s, she lives and teaches in Manchester.

Ann Morley is a recent student of the Manchester College of Adult Education and of the Manchester Open College Federation. Currently 'resting between jobs', she lives in south Manchester.

Liz Stanley with Ann Morley

The Life and Death of Emily Wilding Davison

A Biographical Detective Story

with Gertrude Colmore's *The Life of Emily Davison*

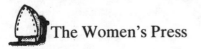 The Women's Press

Published by the Women's Press Limited 1988
A member of the Namara Group
34 Great Sutton Street, London EC1V 0DX

British Library Cataloguing in Publication Data

Stanley, Liz, *1947* –
    The life and death of Emily Wilding Davison.
    1.   England. Women's suffrage movements.
    Davison, Emily Wilding. Biographies
    Rn: Gertrude Weaver   I. Title   II. Morley, Ann
    324.6′23′0924

    ISBN 0-7043-4133-6

Typeset by MC Typeset Ltd, Chatham, Kent
Printed and bound in Great Britain by Cox & Wyman Ltd, Reading

'Thoughts Have Gone Forth Whose Powers Can Sleep No More!
Victory! Victory!'

This book is dedicated with admiration and respect
to the abiding memory
of all the militant feminists
of the Edwardian era

Contents

Preamble

Picture the scene. It is Derby Day Wednesday 4 June 1913 and a tremendous occasion in Edwardian England, one of the public occasions that break everyday routine – like the suffragette marches and demonstrations that have so interested and enlivened people over the last few years in London and many other parts of the country. Thousands of people converge on small, still rural Epsom at the foot of the South Downs: the aristocracy in new-fangled horseless 'cars' and more orderly horse-drawn conveyances, the down-and-out on foot in search of excitement and winnings from races, the great mass of ordinary Edwardians arriving by train, looking for a pleasant day out. The King's horse Anmer is racing; the King himself, George V, and his wife Queen Mary are present.

But some people are here with a more serious political purpose. One suffragette stands in the crowd near Tattenham corner, hoping to sell copies of *The Suffragette*, but is ignored or sneered at by most people. She listens to the sound of the third race in the distance, the sound of the jostling, excited, noisy crowd surrounding her. A familiar face catches her eye, that of a suffragette comrade, also one of the 'militants' but a 'figure' in Women's Social and Political Union circles and rather aloof; not the kind of woman to spend an idle day at the races. Casually, Mary watches her and wonders why on earth she is here. Then, with no sign or warning from the woman's face, she suddenly moves, slips out under the barrier between horses and crowd, and – and what?

Horror-struck, Mary sees the confusion of woman and horses, there are angry shouts and a sudden milling of people on to the race-course. A furious race-goer hits her with one of her own newspapers and pursues her as she rushes off, fearful for her own safety at the hands of angry men thwarted of possible winnings, but more importantly who want to strike back at one of those trouble-making suffragettes.

The militant woman who went out on to the Derby race-course was Emily Wilding Davison; she died of her injuries four days later. The watching suffragette was Mary Richardson, who wrote about that day in a section of her autobiography, *Laugh a Defiance* (1953). Our book is concerned with re-assessing Emily Davison's death and the various circumstances that led up to it. Since it happened, many people have argued about its causes and its consequences, so that now, seventy-five years on, it has become very difficult to strip away all the successive layers of mythologising to see and understand the events themselves.

In 1913 Emily Davison died as a consequence of action she took as a militant suffragette. Fifteen years later, in 1928, women finally achieved complete adult suffrage. Fifty years after that, in 1978, the publisher of this book, The Women's Press, was formed. Therefore 1988 brings with it three important anniversaries for British feminism: the seventy-fifth anniversary of Emily Wilding Davison's death, the sixtieth anniversary of complete women's suffrage, and the tenth anniversary of The Women's Press.

This book came into existence as a twinkle in Ann Morley's eye in spring 1987 because of the impending anniversary of Emily Davison's death. By then having a rather different view of her, Ann was annoyed that Emily should be unremembered by feminists except in terms of what Constance Lytton, a colleague of Emily's, referred to in *Prisons and Prisoners* (1914) as the 'Punch version of a Suffragette'. That is, a stereotypical unattractive badge-festooned spinster mindlessly in love with 'the leaders' and obsessionally concerned with 'the vote and nothing but the vote'. Ann's interest in Emily Davison was infectious: Liz Stanley caught it through various discussions with Ann but particularly after reading Gertrude Colmore's biography of Emily and then a nine-hour stint in Manchester Central Reference Library agog over the pages of *The Suffragette*.

We went to work on the book at high speed, consumed with curiosity. We did so not only in order that it should appear as a commemoration of Emily Davison's death, but also so that the conjunction of this anniversary and the sixtieth anniversary of the achievement of women's suffrage in Britain should not go unnoticed and uncelebrated by contemporary feminists. In its pages we examine some of the misconceptions that exist concerning the nature of Edwardian feminism, misconceptions that have led many people to dismiss militant suffragettes as foolish middle-class women obsessed with the vote and nothing but the vote. While exploring the history of Emily Davison's life, times and death we coincidentally found out about and report on the history of the original British Woman's Press, the publisher of Gertrude Colmore's 1913 biography *The Life of Emily Davison*. Its history is an important one and is symbiotically linked to that of its 'mother' organisation, the Women's Social and Political Union (WSPU).

We have not written – nor did we want to write – a traditional biography of Emily Davison. The form this book takes is unconventional among even feminist biographies. It begins with a reprint of Gertrude Colmore's short biography, now immensely rare. The fact that it was written by Gertrude Colmore and published by the original Woman's Press is, as we will show, a clear demonstration of the totally political response of a large section of British feminism to the completely political nature of Emily's death. A major part of our project in rescuing Emily Wilding Davison from the myths surrounding her memory was to ensure the republication of the original biography of her.

This calculated unconventionality continues through our own biographical assessment of Emily Davison herself, as we explain in our Introduction (see pp. 67–70). We have greatly enjoyed the work we have done for this book; and we are still enjoying it, for the process of finding out continues after this text has been 'finished' for publication purposes. We still have hopes of tracking down material to fill some of the gaps in what we have written, of solving some of the puzzles that remain, and above all of learning yet more about the history of Edwardian feminism and the many courageous and far-sighted women who were active within it. We hope that you will enjoy reading it as much as we have enjoyed writing it.

Perhaps it is useful to state at the outset that this book does not provide a general history of the militant suffragette movement. For those readers unfamiliar with the course of feminist events between 1906 and 1914, we recommend to you Antonia Raeburn's immensely readable *The Militant Suffragettes* (1973) and Andrew Rosen's more academic *Rise Up Women!* (1974). The difference between these two works is an interesting one. Andrew Rosen's book focuses on the machinations of the prime minister, cabinet ministers and members of parliament and on the many ways that WSPU women – particularly the small group of women who constituted its national leadership – attempted to influence them. In contrast – and much closer to our own focus – Antonia Raeburn's book is largely composed of interviews with WSPU women and is concerned with seeing events through their eyes. She has been criticised for this, for dealing with 'mere personalities' rather than the 'important facts'. However, as we shall show, the important facts of the history of the WSPU as an organisation do indeed lie away from the parliamentary machinations that obsessed some of its leadership and many present-day writers.

The most pertinent and interesting aspects of the history of the WSPU lie in the development of a feminist community in Edwardian England, a community organised on a local level throughout the country and concerned with what present-day feminist writing calls personal, rather than merely parliamentary, politics – a concern which can be summed up by the phrase 'the personal is the political'. Keeping in mind the less than overwhelming importance of the parliamentary machine to the most keenly feminist of WSPU women, some important markers of this history are as follows.

The WSPU was founded in Manchester in 1903 by Mrs Emmeline Pankhurst and a small group of other socialist as well as feminist women. It remained small and low key in its activities until October 1905, when Christabel Pankhurst and Annie Kenney decided to interrupt a Manchester election meeting; for committing a 'technical offence' (Christabel politely spat at a policeman), they received the first prison sentences given to feminists. Suddenly the national and local press reported WSPU action and a large number of new members were attracted. The tactic of heckling at election and other party political meetings, being arrested and breaking press silence and so attracting new members was repeated over and over again until the start of the First World War in late summer 1914.

By 1907 the WSPU had grown enormously and attracted much attention, including the grudging approval of the National Union of Women's Suffrage Societies, also originally Manchester based, which was founded in the late 1860s and was a firmly 'constitutional' society. For complex reasons (dealt with in the various histories of the Edwardian feminist movement but which centre on the intransigence and betrayals of socialist men, with some few honourable exceptions), the WSPU leadership moved to a position in which the organisation often opposed socialist as well as Liberal and Conservative men.

From beginning to end the WSPU was a loose coalition of women whose opinions, analyses and actions differed enormously. Early in its history, one group of socialist women felt that a democratic decision-making structure should be adopted. The Pankhursts and their supporters felt strongly that the WSPU should remain under their personal control, and – on a vote at the first and last annual conference in September 1907 – it was their view that prevailed. Many socialist women stayed in the WSPU, but the dissenters left to found the Women's Freedom League.

During its most active life, from 1906 to summer 1914, tactics used by WSPU women changed markedly, from traditionally 'constitutional' activities (like tea meetings and the political wooing of 'important' men) to the development of militancy. In fact what was seen as militancy itself changed in this period, from mass public meetings, demonstrations and marches to hunger-strikes, forcible feeding, window breaking, stone throwing, firing pillar boxes, other acts of arson, and bombings.

Conventionally, such developments are seen as the product of leadership instruction. However, as we shall show, militancy is better understood by reference to personal politics and the development of the feminist community referred to above. And it wasn't only rank-and-file WSPU women who changed; so too did the opinions and actions of the small number of women who constituted its formal leadership: most importantly Mrs Pankhurst, Christabel and their followers, and, after February 1906, Emmeline Pethick-Lawrence. Differences also occurred between the various leaders, of which there are two major indicators. Christabel fled from London following the arrest of other WSPU national staff and leaders in March 1912, setting up as a 'leader over the water' in Paris. Then Emmeline Pethick-Lawrence was effectively banished in her absence later in 1912: the offices were moved, finances reorganised and personnel changed at the command of Mrs Pankhurst, Christabel (in London in disguise for the occasion) and their henchwomen. Other indicators include the marginalisation of both Sylvia and Adela Pankhurst in the organisation.

Historians of Edwardian feminism often see militancy as the product of Pankhurst command, while our reconstruction of the histories of Emily Wilding Davison and her militant comrades shows something quite different. The changing face of militancy was unsought, largely unwelcome and sometimes resisted by the WSPU leadership, and by one or both of the Pankhursts in particular. Militancy, we argue, has to be located in and understood by reference to what one of Walt Whitman's poems calls 'the dear love of comrades'. That is, by close reference to the web of friendship that existed between Emily Davison and her closest feminist friends and comrades.

Although our interest in Emily Davison came before laying hands on a (photo)copy of the fabled Colmore biography, it is fitting that what we say about Emily Davison's life, times and friends should be preceded by what Gertrude Colmore says. Colmore's biography of Emily is a *political* biography, in the sense that it was produced and published – at high speed – to make political capital from Emily's death, to construct it as the martyrdom for 'the cause' that many people had been waiting for. Such a public, feminist death was thought to be bound to occur sooner or later, although a death rather different from Emily's was expected. In addition, Gertrude Colmore's biography, hagiography though it undoubtedly is, remains an important reference point, for it contains the basic source material for all later writers on Emily Davison. Many commentators to date have relied on bowdlerised versions of the basic Colmore facts and on Emily's own potted political biography from the *Suffrage Annual & Women's Who's Who* of 1913, interpreted and used in their own ways.

As we shall show, the Colmore biography excludes much that is important in understanding Emily Davison's life and thus her death. We have used a lot of new evidence in producing this book, perhaps most importantly the Emily Wilding Davison material recently donated to the Fawcett Library. However, this does not mean that the Colmore biography hasn't remained the basic reference point for us too. Indeed, our work points to the fact that Emily Davison's death, the martyred militant's funeral and the Colmore biography became three 'moments' within the last and the most spectacular public display of militant suffragette solidarity. Understanding the political significance of the Colmore biography is thus essential to a proper understanding and appreciation of Emily Davison's life and death.

Liz Stanley and Ann Morley
Blackheddon, near Morpeth
August, 1987

THE LIFE OF
EMILY DAVISON

AN OUTLINE
by G. COLMORE

THE WOMAN'S PRESS
LINCOLN'S INN HOUSE, KINGSWAY, W.C.
1913

THE
LIFE OF EMILY DAVISON

AN OUTLINE

In the north country there is a little grey
town, set in a basin of green hills. One of
these hills bears on and about its summit
remnants of a castle built and destroyed in
bygone days ; and on the shoulder of this
same hill stands an old, old church, in a
churchyard thick grown with yews and
cypresses, with cedar pines and trees and
shrubbery of many kinds.

In that church, on a Sunday in June, in
the year 1913, the burial service was read
over the body of a woman ; a body which
had been carried from the midst of a shouting
multitude to a shelter where death might
come quietly ; which had been borne through
silent crowds along miles of London streets ;
which had been brought, led, and followed by
white-robed figures, to the place where it was
to be laid.

The name of the grey northern town is
Morpeth, and the body brought back to it
from the south was that of its most splendid
daughter, and in that ancient graveyard, on
a slope stretching upward from the church

towards the sky, lies the dead sheath of her who was known in life as Emily Wilding Davison.

The south holds her birthplace, but she came of a northern race, and the north showed itself in her energy, her endurance, her untiring purpose. Some kinship there was between her and that other Emily of the north, moorland bred, genius dowered, the Emily who seared with hot iron the poisoned wound in her hand made by the bite of a mad dog. Emily Davison might have done that ; hers was the same determined will, the same unshrinking courage that lived in Emily Brontë; and hers, too, the strong sense of duty and the religious temperament inherent in all the Brontë sisters. But in those sisters there was a touch of melancholy, of shrinking from contact with the outer world, of aloofness, entirely lacking in the woman who loved the life she was prepared to lose, whose capacity for enjoyment was unusually keen, who was able to throw herself whole-heartedly into each and every pleasure that came her way. Perhaps in the Brontës there was some of the loneliness of the moors on which they were bred and which they so passionately loved, a little of the ruggedness, a touch of the spirit of solitude. In the country to which Emily Davison belonged there is nothing rugged, and little that is lonely. It is a country of wide spaces, of undulating fields, of far horizons ; remote but not desolate, solitary but not bare ; a country not unlike in character and atmosphere to the country in which her earliest years were passed.

She was born on the 11th of October, 1872, on the outskirts of that London in which so much of the drama of her life was to be played ; at Blackheath, whither the Davison family had come from Morpeth, not long before her birth ; but while she was still a baby they moved from Blackheath to a house near the village of Sawbridgeworth, in the border country of Hertfordshire and Essex. Gaston House, where Emily Davison spent her childhood, is a Georgian house three storeys in height, with tall, spacious rooms, and on its red brick front the kindly look that some old houses have. Here and in the garden that surrounds it Emily lived and learned and played through the first nine years of her life. Here, near the head of the stairs, is the nursery which was the home of her babyhood, and here, between the stairhead and the nursery door, the bit of wall against which, with arms folded behind her, legs stretched outwards and firmly planted feet, she many a time stood, defying authority.

Authority in the shape of Nurse would call to her : " Miss Emily, do come in and be a good girl."

And back the answer would go : " I don't want to be good."

To be good when goodness meant merely submission to the powers that be was never her way. Later on she submitted willingly to authority that had reason and right behind it ; but always, all through her life, when right had no representative but might, she stood with her back to the wall with feet firmly planted.

Emily was the youngest but one of the band of children at Gaston House, Ethel, who died in childhood, being the baby of the family ; and during the latter's short life, these two were close companions. Even in her earliest years Emily's religious temperament showed itself, and she and Ethel, after they were put to bed, never would go to sleep till they had sung a hymn together. Their mother, standing on the stairs that led to the nurseries, would listen to the two little creatures singing in their cribs, and the hymn beginning " We are but little children weak," was the one she listened to most often.

> " We know the Holy Innocents
> Laid down for him their infant life,
> And Martyrs brave and patient Saints
> Have stood for Him in fire and strife."

The spirit that was glad in the child singing those words was the spirit that sang later within prison walls.

Almost from the time she could speak Emily was the leader of the other children, and also the emissary sent on missions of demand or diplomacy. When cakes or sweets were desired it was Emily who was sent to ask for them, and constantly the little messenger would go downstairs to her mother with a request for " weet, weet," the nearest approach to " sweet " that her lips could compass. So often did this happen that " Weet " became one of the several names she went by. The last postcard she sent to her mother was signed with that name.

Another of her names, coined originally as a term of ignominy and reproach, was Pem. It happened, during a summer when flies were especially numerous and vast numbers in the house had been slain by fly papers, that one day it occurred to the children to bury all the dead winged bodies. There was to be a sort of military funeral, a procession, with soldiers. Playing at soldiers, organising battles and processions were amongst Emily's favourite games. She cared nothing for dolls ; it was the martial rather than the maternal spirit which was dominant in her childhood, nor was she devoid of the disciplinary instincts of the martinet. The procession was about to start, when lo ! it was discovered that the soldiers had no flags, and were not in correct marching order. That must not be ; flags they must have and right ceremonial. And then arose conflict. What did it matter for flies ? said the other children. They would not wait till flags were manufactured, nor were they prepared to

7

march save in a straggling fashion. Then they must march without Emily : the thing must be properly done or not done at all ; on that occasion, as on all others, processions or anything else in which she took part must be correctly carried out. So Emily stayed behind. Usually her will prevailed, but on this occasion the joint forces of opposition prevailed against her, and the funeral was conducted in a fashion which, as she could not prevent it, she refused to countenance. These forces were very cross with her : her absence spoiled the game, and their resentment showed itself in the invention of a name intended to express the utmost displeasure and contempt. Pem sounds harmless enough, but it seems to have meant much to them and to her, and to have given adequate expression to the anger of the inventors. The quarrel was soon made up, but somehow the name stuck, and Pem, long since purged of opprobrium, became one of Emily's nicknames, one of the many names by which she was known and loved.

She was a high-spirited child, daring and somewhat mischievous. A friend with whose family she used to stay describes her as having been " a regular pickle." " She used to come and stay with us," she says, " at our country home in Lancashire. It was a large, old-fashioned, rambling place, with extensive grounds and plenty of outhouses, providing endless amusement for us all as children.

Emily first came as quite a child, and I remember her full of high spirits and daring, delighting in treading on forbidden ground, but with nothing mean or small about her. Always very affectionate and impulsive, and, needless to say, a most intelligent child." Passionate she was as a child, but never sulky, and she hated being teased, which, as she was one of a large family, happened not too rarely. Of a very sensitive nature, environment affected her strongly, and always, all her life, her spirit rose against oppression.

Emily's education was begun at Gaston House under a resident governess, but when she was about eleven years of age her parents gave up their country home and went to live in London, where she attended Miss Crookshank's day school for a time. For about a year she was in France at Dunkerque with her sister; then she returned to England, and when she was thirteen years old began her attendance at the Kensington High School, where she remained, with the exception of a year spent at Lausanne for the purpose of learning French, till 1891. Miss Hitchcock, who was Head Mistress at that time, gives a vivid sketch of the new pupil.

" I well remember her coming with her father, who was evidently very devoted to her and very much afraid she might be overworked. She was rather a delicate looking child, fair-haired and without much colour, but with bright, intelligent eyes, and a half shy, half confident way of looking up with her head a little on one side and smiling at one which won my heart at once. She seemed, I remember, delighted to be coming to school and to be with other girls—and that is my impression of her all the time she was there—her pleasure in her work and her interest in everything that went on." This impression of keen interest and of constant appetite for work, Emily seems to have produced on all about her, and she was popular alike with teachers and taught. The testimony of those who knew her at that time shows that she was easy to get on with, placid in temper, free from moods, and so was on good terms with her schoolfellows ; while her work, conscientious and good, and her law-abiding disposition won the approval of the mistresses. For she was law-abiding in those days, was law-abiding by nature, " the very reverse," says one of her school friends, " of the aggressive character generally expected of the suffragette—made or in the making."

Not that the character of the suffragette was discussed by Emily and her school friends. There were no suffragettes in those days, for the question of Woman's Suffrage was still an academic one, and the topics chiefly of interest to Emily and her companions were those connected with work and school. Her chief friend at that time has no recollection of discussing woman's rights with her or any public question. Far more interesting to them both was Chaucer's *Knight's Tale*, which they were both studying, and from which Emily derived another of her names. " The faire Emelye " she was always called from that time on by this friend and a few others, her hair, which was fair and very pretty, making the name appropriate.

Literature was one of her delights, and she was keenly appreciative of all that was inspiring and beautiful. " I remember her as a very gentle-mannered girl," says Miss Hitchcock. " She did not attract as much attention or inspire as many hopes as to her future career as other and more brilliant girls who were her contemporaries. But she had a way of coming out better in examinations than we expected, and her essays showed thought and originality above the average. She was an interesting pupil, quickly stirred over passages in history and literature that appealed to her sense of the noble and the beautiful. Under a quiet, unassuming exterior there was a great fund of enthusiasm, and a surprising power of steady and persistent work. . . ."

But Emily's work did not by any means absorb all her interest. She was not only a student, conscientious and keen, but also an ardent cyclist and swimmer, and she skated and danced enthusiastically. Her swimming was exceptionally good ; later on she gained a gold medal at a swimming championship at the Chelsea Baths, and once, when she was at Brighton, a champion swimmer offered to give her lessons for nothing if she would become a professional. At Cromer one season she was the last of the bathers, bathing well on into November. She was never a weakling ; strong in body and in mind, her energy was unflagging, and her interests wide as well as keen. Amongst those interests was the theatre, to which she went constantly even as a girl, and here again "her infinite variety" showed itself. The friend who was her constant companion had no liking for musical comedy—was, in fact, bored by it. Not so Emily. " My tastes are far more catholic than yours," she declared, " for I can enjoy a musical comedy as much as a Shakespeare play or a Bernard Shaw or a Gilbert Murray."

It was with this friend that she went to pay a visit to an old schoolfellow who had gone to Holloway College, and the visit created in her a keen desire to go there as a student. To desire with Emily Davison was to set herself to obtain what she desired, and she worked hard to reach her end, doing better work, both at this time and later, than some of her more obviously brilliant companions. She passed the Higher Certificate Examination of the Oxford and Cambridge Joint Board while still at school, and in 1891, when she was nineteen, she obtained a bursary at Holloway College. A letter written in this year, a regular schoolgirl's

letter, shows the simplicity and affectionate-
ness of her nature, her keen interest in
school life, her loving admiration of her
teachers. There was no conflict between
Emily Davison and the authorities in those
days.

At Holloway College Emily studied as
diligently as she had studied at Kensington
High School. She was working for the
Oxford Honour School in English Literature. She seems to have been very happy in
those days; in beautiful surrroundings, with
congenial companionships, doing work in
which she was keenly interested. Did she
ever, when at Holloway College, pass
Holloway Gaol ? Did she ever, if she passed
it, think of the women within ? Was there
ever in her mind the faintest presage that she
was to be prisoned behind its walls ? Probably as to any presentiment of what was to
come the answer is no. Healthy, happy-
minded girl that she was, the tragedies of the
outer world formed as yet no part of her
consciousness ; pain and conflict can hardly
have been in her scheme of things, nor the
thought of them have clouded her eager
outlook upon life. Hidden from her surely
was any faintest picture of punishment cells,
of iron staircase, of hours of lonely endurance,
silenced any far-off slightest echo of the
cries of fellow-prisoners, the hiss of rushing
water, the march of many feet—or the sound
of horses' hoofs galloping over turf.

Emily was only half-way through her course at Holloway College, had been there but two years, when her father died. In a letter written on February 15th, 1893, she gives a long account of the funeral, and the taking of the body to Morpeth. There are sentences in it which might have been written by her friends about another funeral twenty years later.

" We . . . saw the coffin go off, covered with most lovely flowers, to King's Cross. . . . The church is very old-fashioned, with a lich gate. . . ." It was the first time, evidently, that she had been to Morpeth, the first time she had seen the church which she was to make historical. In that same letter she writes :—

" To-day we have been very busy, and I have been out for Mamma. She has decided that I am to return *to-morrow* to college. It is very hard to leave them all . . . but what can one do ? Mamma has to pay £20 a term for me, and it must not be wasted. I do not know whether I can stay on after this term, as we do not know how matters are yet, so I must make the best of this term. Mamma is *very* anxious to keep me at college for my exam. if it is possible."

It proved not to be possible, and Emily, with her usual courage and determination, left the college and took a post as resident governess, with a definite agreement that she should have free time in the evening for private work. She read hard for about a year, borrowing note books from college friends who were still attending lectures, saved enough money to pay for one term at St. Hugh's Hall immediately before the examination, and came out with a First Class. The need for hard study was over now ; but Emily was not happy until she was working at something besides routine work, and after a time she began to read for the London degree, with the result that she graduated with honours at London University.

For a time after passing her Oxford examination she tried public school work, but in this she does not appear to have been very happy. She found it hard to tolerate laziness and stupidity, and the discipline seems to have been a difficulty—a curious one, considering her will power and force of character. In any case public school work proved uncongenial, and after a time she gave it up and went to a private school at Worthing, which suited her better, and where she was successful in preparing pupils for the Cambridge Higher Local Examinations. Later on she took a private post, and remained with one family for six years.

Her period of teaching lasted altogether for thirteen years, from 1893 till 1906, when she found that the carrying on of her profession and devotion to the woman's movement were incompatible. During these years she continued to visit Miss Hitchcock, with whom she remained friends to the last, Miss Hitchcock's affection for her former pupil persisting in spite of her disapproval of Emily's militant career. Her own words are :—

" Although I did not share Emily's views as to the line she felt impelled to take in the last few years, my affection for her, and my appreciation of her character, were unaltered."

Miss Hitchcock's testimony with regard to that character is remarkable, showing forth its strength, its joyousness, its utter lack of any morbid element. All through the years when Emily went " fairly often " to see her, there was always the same bright look and happy, cheerful attitude towards life. " I never heard her complain or express anxiety about her own future or that of her mother. I never heard her utter a word against anyone under whom or with whom she worked, and no one ever had less thought of adopting a ' misunderstood ' pose, or the rôle of the neglected governess. On the contrary, she spoke of her affection for her pupils and of the kindness she received from their parents."

Yet there must have been for her in a sense, and that a very important sense, much loneliness in the home of her pupils ; for in that home there was no sympathy with the views which day by day she held more strongly ; the parents whom she mentioned only to speak of their kindness were opposed to the cause which she longed to serve. She felt that it would not be honourable to influence her pupils in favour of the suffrage as their mother disapproved of the movement, and how could she speak to them of it without influencing them ? So she was forced into silence about what was rapidly becoming the chief interest in her life.

It was the distorted accounts of suffrage proceedings in the newspapers which first aroused Emily Davison's interest in the cause which she was to serve so well. When the W.S.P.U. was beginning to be talked about she read in the papers reports of what members had said at meetings. These reports she could not believe to be accurate, so, out of curiosity at first, and to verify her impressions, she began attending meetings. She found, as she had thought must be the case, that the speakers were entirely misrepresented, and her interest and ardour quickly grew.

In 1906 she became a member of the Women's Social and Political Union, but at first, owing to the obligations of her then position, she could not take as large a share in its activities as she wished to do. Yet work of some kind she succeeded in accomplishing, and when she had been about eighteen months in the Union we find her in an official position. On Sunday, June 21st,

1908, was held the first of the many great processions organised by the Women's Social and Political Union ; a sevenfold procession on this occasion, seven battalions of women converging from seven main starting points at Hyde Park and holding there a monster meeting. Emily was chief steward at the Great Central Station, her duty and that of her companions being to meet everyone of the trains that bore adherents to the Cause from seventy towns to Marylebone, to welcome the arriving women, and to hand them on to the marshals who met them outside the station. She was glad and happy in the task ; one who shared it testifies to her brightness and energy, and to her keen regret that she was obliged to return to her pupils before the whole work of the day was done.

It was about this time that she gave up the post she had held for six years, and went to teach in a family in Berkshire. Here she seems to have had considerable freedom in various directions, and was in beautiful surroundings ; but she was too far away from what for her was the pulse of life ; her interests were in the world of outside effort and public work, and she confessed to a friend that she would rather live in the ugliest house in London than in the loveliest place in the country. Some verses that she wrote, whether written then or later, express what at this time she undoubtedly felt :—

Oh, London! How I feel thy magic spell
    Now I have left thee, and amid the woods
Sit lonely. Here I know I love thee well,
    Conscious of all the glamour of thy moods.
But it is otherwise amid thy bounds!
    Thou art an ocean of humanity!
Embarked on which I lose my soul in sounds
    That thunder in mine ear. The vanity
And ceaseless struggle stifle doubt and fear
    Until I cry, bemused by the strife,
" The centre of the universe is here!
    This is the hub, the very fount of life."

The centre of the universe was most certainly for her where the struggle for freedom
waxed most strenuous, and it was not long
before she launched her life upon that
" ocean of humanity " in which the outer
form of it was to perish.

In truth the call had come ; a call which
caused her to put aside all self-interest, all
personal ambition, all claims and hopes
which stood in the way of its behests ; a call
which constrained her to sell the cloak of a
secure livelihood and buy the sword of revolt ;
a call which to her ears was divine. For in
Emily Davison were certain of those qualities
of character and temperament which, when
combined, form what Lord Rosebery has
called a practical mystic. Innately religious,
with keenly and nobly conceived ideals and
an imagination touched by the spirit of
devotion, she was as fully convinced that she
was called by God, not only to work but also
to fight for the cause she had espoused, as was

Joan of Arc when she led the army of France. "She always said very long prayers," is the testimony of a friend who was much with her in her militant days, "and her Bible was always by her bedside." "That she was heart and soul in the movement," says one who had known her from childhood, "no one could doubt, or that she looked upon her share in it as a special work to which she had been called. . . . I regretted the line she took . . . but I was convinced that she believed herself to be obeying a direct call." "I never do any of the things" (i.e., acts of militancy) Emily told her mother, "except under the Influence."

In such wise spoke Joan of Arc, in such wise Cromwell, in such wise St. Paul. There are those who declare that St. Paul saw no light on his way to Damascus, and that when he said "I am not mad, most noble Felix," he uttered an obvious untruth ; there are those who maintain that there is no vision save of the earth, earthy, and that in the poet's eye rolling in fine frenzy is nought of the perception of the seer ; there are those who would substitute always the maniac's straight waistcoat for the martyr's crown. Nevertheless the vision persists, the martyr's memory outlives the carpings of the crowd, and the blood of reformers is the seed of the great movements of the world.

The call having come, it was not long before Emily Davison found it impossible to serve two masters, and the service she clung to was not that which ensured material well-being. In less than a year after the day on which she acted as steward she gave up private teaching and made the cause of woman's freedom the first object of her gifts, her energy, her untiring devotion.

On March 20th, 1909, there was a deputation to Mr. Asquith, following a resolution passed at the Free Trade Hall, Manchester, on the previous Wednesday. Emily Davison was one of the women arrested for making an attempt to see the Prime Minister, and, refusing either to give an undertaking not to repeat what was called her offence or to be bound over for six months, she was sentenced to one month's imprisonment. In *Votes for Women* of April 2nd she is described as having taken an active part in the London campaign and being a valued worker in the cause.

That was her first imprisonment ; the second followed close upon it. On July 30th there was a meeting at Limehouse at which Mr. Lloyd George spoke in advocacy of the Budget. No women were allowed in the hall except two who were on the platform, and the protests against the Government's policy in regard to women were made by men. But women were outside, and, while their supporters within were set upon by the stewards, interrupted the meeting and distracted the audience by suffrage battle cries which came in a volume of sound through the windows.

Emily was amongst those who were arrested and imprisoned, and who adopted the hunger strike, instituted in the preceding month by Miss Wallace Dunlop, as a protest against the refusal to treat suffragist prisoners as political offenders. A letter written on August 12th, when she was staying with her mother at Longhorsley, describes her experiences, and shows the buoyancy as well as the determination of her spirit, the simplicity of her character, and the pleasure she took in little things—even in picture postcards— which was characteristic of her all her days. Speaking of the hunger-strike, she says :

Did you read about it? We went outside Lloyd George's Budget Meeting at Lime-house, and protested at women being kept out, etc. I was busy haranguing the crowd when the police came up and arrested me. We were charged next day at the Thames Police Court. I and Mrs. Leigh got the longest sentences, *i.e.*, two months, the rest mostly got two weeks. We all resolved on the " Hunger-strike " and mutiny if we were not treated as 1st class prisoners. We asked for the Governor. He told us we were to be 2nd class (they *refused to* tell us at the Court), but that if we would go quietly to our cells we could keep our clothes. But refused to be anything but 1st class. Then they took us off one by one after a struggle. When I was shut in the cell I at once smashed seventeen panes of glass. *Please,* if you are asked why we did this, say, because we object to the fact that the windows can never be opened, and the ventilation is bad.

Then they rushed me into another cell, in which everything was fixed. I broke seven panes of that window, to the matron's utter astonishment, as I had a *hammer*. I could not have done it otherwise, and I don't think any of the others were able to do that. It took some time. Then they forcibly undressed me and left me sitting in a prison chemise. I sang the second verse of " God Save the King," with " Confound their politics " in it! The doctor came in to sound me, and I refused to be sounded. Then I was dressed in prison clothes and taken into one of the worst cells, very dark, and with double doors. Then the real grind began. I fasted 124 hours, and was then released. I lost 1½ stone and much flesh. I felt very weak at first, but I am pulling up rapidly now. My mother is making me feed up hard, and I am being very lazy. What did you think of me? I suppose you are in Switzerland now? Do send me some picture postcards. . . . Please write soon

to your

loving and rebellious friend.

The letter is signed with the name from the *Knight's Tale*, " Emelye."

A little incident of this imprisonment, given in her own words, is strongly characteristic of her. " In the dark punishment cell, to my delight, I found on my wall Mrs. Dove-Willcox's name and ' *Dum spiro spero*.' I added mine and ' Rebellion against tyrants is obedience to God.'" The key to Emily Davison's militant career lies in those words which she wrote on the walls of Holloway.

In August she was " being very lazy " at Longhorsely; in September she was again in prison, again went through the hunger strike. At a Budget demonstration at the White City, Manchester, she and four companions managed to elude the vigilance of the police and broke glass panes in the Concert Hall, by means of stone throwing. Her sentence was £5 costs, and 4s. for damage done, or two months' imprisonment Needless to say, she elected to go to prison, and with her fellow offenders was consigned to Strangeways Gaol, where they all mutinied and hunger struck. An attempt was made to overcome their resistance by means of handcuffing and specially severe treatment, one of them being put into a straight waistcoat ; but the spirit of the prisoners remained unbroken, and they were all released on the evening of September 8th, after two days' confinement.

Again Emily did not give herself much time in which to recover from the effects of the hunger strike and the prison treatment. On the 9th of October Mr. Lloyd George was to speak at Newcastle. The visit was not to pass without protest, and on the evening of the 8th twelve women met together to decide on their plan of campaign. Emily Davison was one of these women and Lady Constance Lytton was another ; and it was arranged, in settling the various acts of protest, that these two were to work together.

Saturday afternoon came. A large square in front of the Theatre was barricaded and guarded by police. Mr. Lloyd George was conveyed to the meeting in Sir Walter Runciman's car by back streets and reached his destination unseen by the crowd, after which Sir Walter proceeded from the Theatre ·to St. George's Hall. As he was passing the offices of the Newcastle Breweries two women rushed forward ; one of them, Lady Constance Lytton, threw a stone at the car; Emily Davison had no time to send a second stone after the first before she, as well as her companion, was arrested. But the first missile had reached its aim, which was the car, not its occupants, and on the paper in which it was wrapped were Emily's favourite words, " Rebellion against tyrants is obedience to God."

On Monday the two prisoners appeared at the Police Court with six others, after two days in the cells. Lady Constance, who had thrown the stone with the direct object of challenging the Government to treat her as they had treated Mrs. Leigh for a similar offence, was charged with assaulting Sir Walter Runciman, and, refusing to find sureties for good behaviour, was sentenced to a month's imprisonment ; Emily, charged with attempted assault, was released.

Not for long. A little over a fortnight later Mr. Runciman was speaking at Radcliffe at a Budget meeting, a meeting from which women were excluded. As no protest against the Government's policy with regard to the Franchise question could therefore be made within the meeting, a protest was made without, and Emily and three other women were arrested for breaking the windows of the Post Office and the Liberal Club.

Emily had been through the hunger-strike more than once ; she was now to endure the torture of forcible feeding, to which the Government had resorted since her last imprisonment. In connection with the arrest at Radcliffe she is described as " one of the most devoted voluntary workers in the Union, and has given up her whole life for the cause." It was true ; she had given everything she had to give, her talents, her time, her courage, her career, and given all ungrudgingly ; entering fully into the spirit of the Union to which she belonged ; a spirit which asks nothing from its members, but accepts all gifts and all sacrifices ; which neither condemns those who withhold nor praises those who give ; which counts service rendered as rendered neither to its leaders nor itself, but to the cause for which all stand ; which sees the reward of the worker in the greatness of the work.

Emily, when she left Strangeways Gaol in September, had a foreboding that she had not seen the last of it. The foreboding was soon to be fulfilled ; on October 21st she was once more shut up in one of its solitary cells. She, together with her fellow-prisoners, had begun the hunger-strike in Bury Police Court, and the day after she entered the Manchester Prison she was subjected to forcible feeding. It was in the evening that the matron, two doctors, and five or six wardresses entered her cell. The senior doctor sounded her; then—

" I am going to feed you by force," he said.

Emily protested that such an operation performed against her will was illegal. The doctor's only reply was that it was no concern of his.

Grasped by the wardresses, she was forced down on the bed, while the senior doctor, seizing her by the hair—the fair, abundant hair that was her chief beauty—pulled her head by it violently on to the pillow.

" The scene which followed," said Emily, when speaking of it afterwards, " will haunt me with its horror all my life, and is almost indescribable. While they held me flat, the elder doctor tried all round my mouth with a steel gag to find an opening. On the right side of my mouth two teeth are missing; this gap he found, pushed in the horrid instrument, and prised open my mouth to its widest extent. Then a wardress poured liquid down my throat out of a tin enamelled cup. What it was I could not say, but there was some medicament which was foul to the last degree. As I would not swallow the stuff

27

and jerked it out with my tongue, the doctor pinched my nose and somehow gripped my tongue with the gag. The torture was barbaric."

That first ordeal took place on Friday evening ; on Monday Emily was put into an adjoining cell, while the window she had broken in the one to which she was first consigned was mended. Entering, she saw that this cell contained two plank beds, the bed belonging to it and the one they had taken from her that morning. Instantly she perceived that here was the means to barricade the door, and as soon as the wardress was gone, quick as thought and very quietly, she put the two beds lengthways one beyond the other across the floor of the cell. A space of about two feet remained between the second bed and the wall ; the stool, legs upwards, filled it, and the wedge not being quite firm, her two slippers and a hairbrush were jammed in to make it quite secure. On the only doubtful spot, the place where the two beds joined, she sat down, and, having piled up the table and mattress to add to the weight, quietly waited.

Presently the wardress returned, unlocked the door, and found it would not move. The spy-hole revealed the reason, and Emily was implored to open. She smiled and said, " No."

All the afternoon she sat on her barricade. People came again and again alternately begging and threatening, people who did not know Emily Davison. An attempt was made to prise open the door, and then came a man in authority.

" Get off the planks ! "

No answer, no movement.

" Davison, if you don't get off those planks .and open the door we shall turn the hose-pipe on you."

Years ago a little child had stood with her back to the wall, hands behind her, feet firmly planted. "Do come and be good!" authority had pleaded, and the answer had gone back : " I don't want to be good." The woman's back was against the wall now, very firm were her feet, she was determined that in the prison sense of the words she would not " be good." She sat motionless and calm and silent.

There was a ladder at the window, a crash of glass, and through the breach made, the nozzle of a hose-pipe. It took some time to fix the pipe ; when it was fixed they gave her one more chance, those people who did not know Emily Davison nor the spirit of the Union. Then came the punishment. At first the stream went over her head ; she took hold of the bed boards and sat firm. The course of the stream was altered and came upon her full force, with power that seemed terrific, cold as ice. " I had to hold on," she said, " like grim death." It seemed as if it lasted for an age, that icy flow; it actually did last for something like a quarter of an hour, full and strong upon her ; and still the back of her spirit was against the wall, and the feet of her will were immovable.

At last the operator paused, and a voice called. " Stop ! " it said. " No more, no more."

Authority had done its worst and failed. After all the door must be burst open. But, if it fell, it would fall on the prisoner ; the men outside knew it, so did the woman within. Even at that time Emily and many others had conceived the idea that life would have to be sacrificed before the cause was won; and as she waited, watching the door, fascinated but not afraid, the thought in her mind was that the moment for the sacrifice had come. But the time was not yet.

They called to her to move off the plank, and she did not move ; the door gave, and she did not move. But hands caught it before it fell, and as the gap widened a male warder rushed in, saying, as he seized the prisoner : " You ought to be horsewhipped for this."

The water—six inches deep it was—rushed out into the corridor. Emily was hurried into her former cell, where her clothes were torn off her ; she was wrapped in blankets, and then carried off in an invalid chair to the hospital. A hot bath, bed between blankets with a hot bottle, and wondering wardresses commenting on her iron determination.

And after that she was forcibly fed again, and it was the nasal tube that was used now ; up one nostril it goes and down into the throat ; if it does not go down properly the doctor pushes it down with his hand. No wonder, when they made the prisoner get up the next morning, that they had to put her back to bed again. There she stayed till Thursday, when she was made to get up and go out for exercise. But the limit of bodily endurance had been reached : she must not die on the authorities' hands—on Thursday afternoon she was released.

Coming out of prison she found that the story of the hose-pipe was known all over England, and had been brought up in Parliament—to her surprise, as she had feared all news of her and her fellow-prisoners had been suppressed. " Is Right beginning to prevail over Might at last ? " she wondered. No, not yet ; and now that she is dead, still not yet.

Something had been done : Mr. Keir Hardie asked questions in the House of Commons ; Mr. Snowden suggested that the members of the Visiting Committee should be removed from their offices as Justices of the Peace ; Councillor James Johnson, one of the Committee, moved a resolution of protest stating that as a Justice of the Peace he refused to uphold the action of his colleagues; while throughout the period of incarceration several protests had been made in the neighbourhood of the prison, the number of persons present one day being estimated by the *Manchester Guardian* at between nine and ten thousand. Yet in the following January we find Mr. H. Gladstone vigorously commending the policy of Might trampling upon Right, and writing to the officials of Strangeways Gaol as follows :—

The Commissioners are desired by the Secretary of State to express their appreciation of the way in which you, the medical officer, have carried out your trying and difficult duties in connection with the Suffragist prisoners during the last few weeks. The Secretary of State observes :—" A difficult period has been got through most satisfactorily, owing to the efficiency of the prison service and the carefulness and the good sense shown by the staff." In conveying this message of commendation the Commissioners desire to express their commendation of the tact, care, humanity, and firmness with which this new and difficult problem has been and is being handled by all concerned.

In that same month, January, 1910, Emily Davison brought an action against the local Visiting Justices of Strangeways Gaol in respect of the " tact, care, humanity and firmness " with which she had been handled by means of the hose-pipe. The case was heard on Monday the 10th, but not decided, Judge Parry reserving judgment. On the 19th he pronounced in Emily's favour, awarding damages to the amount of forty shillings and costs on the higher scale, and the illegal

32

character of the Justices' action was thus declared. But the treatment of women in prison was continued on the lines which had won the strong approval of the Secretary of State ; Emily's colleague at Newcastle had been subjected, as Jane Warton, to the intensest suffering ; and it was not long before Emily felt herself called upon to make another protest against the attitude and actions of the Government. This time her design was to penetrate to the interior of the House of Commons and to ask Mr. Asquith why, when he was denouncing the action of the Lords, he would not make the House of Commons representative by giving votes to women taxpayers, and why, before attempting to reform the House of Lords, he did not set his own house in order.

The attempt failed, but the courage, coolness, and endurance involved in it are characteristic of its author's indomitable will. Her experiences are best described in her own words :—

On Saturday last I entered Old Palace Yard at exactly 2.40 p.m. behind two ladies and went up the stairs into the King's Robing Room. Then I passed in with the crowd into the Royal Gallery, the Princes' Chamber, and the House of Lords.

When we moved into the Great Central Hall I saw to my joy a little passage out beyond it, and went with the people at right angles to the House of Commons' corridor. There were doors all round it with " Private " on them. A man passed through one and gave me an idea. As the constable on duty was engaged in conversation, and while the other people were leaving the hall, I tried one of the doors. It gave! I went through. It gave a tiny click, and I was beyond the part which the public were allowed to visit. I stood one moment expecting to be seen or stopped, but as no one came I quietly stepped across to a corridor. In the distance through some glass doors I saw a policeman, but luckily he was not looking my way. In the wall I saw a little glass window with a knob, and when I opened it I looked into a dark place which was very hot, and found it was the heating apparatus of the Houses. I got in and closed the window. There was a series of ladders going up higher and higher into the tower. I climbed up the first with difficulty, as the place was narrow, and reached the first platform. I found two fairly firm planks across a pair of rafters, and as it looked dangerous higher and almost impossible to climb, I took up my abode on one side of this platform and stayed there.

Then came a period of hideous, awful waiting. The time wore away so slowly, for I had nothing to do but think and read my guide to the Houses of Parliament. I was terribly afraid of being discovered, especially as I had a cold which I could not altogether check with lozenges. It was almost overpoweringly hot. The only provisions I had were two bananas and some chocolate. The latter and the lozenges, together with the heat, gradually made me thirsty. I was tired and yet in too uncomfortable a position to sleep. I was also afraid of tumbling over into the well below. Luckily, about 7 o'clock some of the pipes were turned off, and I even began to feel cold, so that I put on my jacket again and huddled up.

The place was indescribably filthy. Years of dirt and dust lay on everything. My face, clothes and head were begrimed. Every now and again with great care I stood up to allay the aching of my bones. Big Ben kept me informed of the slow progress of time, and occasionally I heard the footsteps of some distant watchman.

At last, about 4 o'clock, morning light began to dawn, and I was truly thankful. Hour by hour passed on, till about 7 o'clock the hot pipes were turned on again. As the day wore on and the heat increased, my sufferings from thirst became so intense that I felt that even if I risked being seized I must descend and look for water. It was the first time that I had left my perch.

At 1.45 I descended. Arrived at the bottom I opened the glass window cautiously and looked out. No one was about. To my joy I saw just below the window a tap with a little tin dish below it, and " Cold " printed above it. I climbed out, and as all was silent, eagerly drank some water. It was indescribably comforting. I rubbed some over my begrimed face and hands. I dare not stay, so swallowing as much as I could of the blessed water I crept back into the hiding-place and up the shaft. After that I felt capable of waiting on for days, if necessary. I dozed occasionally, and listened for the Abbey afternoon service bells. Later on, however, I had to go down again for another drink. Four, five, and six o'clock struck, and once more I felt the need of water. I descended, alas for the last time. I drank of the cool, blessed water eagerly. Then I noticed that as the dish was narrow and flat a good deal of water was spilt on the floor, and fervently hoped no one would pass that way.

I had just returned to my niche when I heard steps and saw light, for the evening was closing in. I drew back as far as I could, but, of course, the water attracted the watchman's eyes. He opened the door and looked in, and there he saw me.

What I must have appeared to be I cannot say—a terrible object no doubt. The poor constable was terror-stricken, so that he nearly dropped his lantern. He trembled violently, and called out, " What is it? " He banged the window to, and then he seized his whistle and blew it shrilly. Still trembling, he opened the door again and yelled " Come out ! " When I descended he gripped me hard and drew me out of the passage, and there at last appeared another constable, very much astonished.

After I had washed I was taken quietly to Cannon Row by the station passage, and had a meal which was brought to me by the matron, while they sent in every direction to find a friend who would bail me out, and at last, about 9.30, a constable came in and told me that I was free to go. I could hardly believe it, but found that the authorities had decided not to prosecute me. It appears that I could not have been tried in a Police Court, but would have to appear before the House of Commons itself; this is probably the reason I was not prosecuted. I went back to my lodgings to recover cleanliness and ordinary comfort. Such was my visit to the House of Commons !

But Emily's energies were not confined to deeds designated militant. At this time, namely, in April, 1910, she was employed by the Union and contributed articles of various kinds to its official organ. Amongst her contributions during this year is one describing a megaphone parade in which she took part, articles on Florence Nightingale, on Elizabeth Fry, on Hannah More, and on the Japan-British Exhibition. Never till the end of her life did she lose her interest in writing, in literature, and in study ; never, except when reduced to exhaustion by prison severities, her physical energy, never her power of enjoyment. But always all other interests were subordinate to that cause which she upheld in private as in public, defending all that was done in its name, refusing ever to condemn or to brook condemnation.

There was truce that summer between the Government and the militant suffragists. On the 18th of June all the Women's Suffrage Societies joined in a monster procession, proving to the world how great was the desire for the vote, how keen was the interest in the Bill for which Mr. Asquith had promised facilities. Five days later Mr. Asquith made a most unsatisfactory statement in the House with regard to these facilities. Emily found herself unable to let what seemed to her an insult to women pass without protest, and took action on her own initiative. On the evening of the Prime Minister's pronouncement she broke two panes of glass in the Crown Office with pieces of chalk to which were attached messages of warning. She was fined £5 or a month's imprisonment, choosing, of course, the latter ; but her fine was paid without her knowledge or permission, and she was once more at liberty.

She was at liberty for a time ; and during that time there were some peaceful days, days passed at Longhorsley, where always her holidays were spent with that mother between whom and herself there was an unbreakable bond of sympathy ; who knew, with strange knowledge, coming from within, when Emily was engaged in active warfare ; whose delight was to welcome, to tend and to make much of her in the intervals of leisure and of peace. But of leisure and of peace there was but small measure for Emily from the day she joined the Woman's Movement to the day when consciousness left her physical body on Epsom racecourse. Joan of Arc's famous words : " Fight on and God will give the Victory," were alive in her heart by the side of those words she had chosen for her motto, and she could not long abstain from active work for the cause whose spirit and whose exigencies might well be expressed in Garibaldi's exhortation to his soldiers: "Fortune, who betrays us to-day, will smile on us to-morrow. I offer no pay. I offer insult and abuse and pain and loneliness and loss of friends and the hatred and anger of men. Let him who loves his cause in his heart and not with his lips only, follow me."

In the service of that cause Emily was soon to suffer anew. On Friday, November 18th, Mr. Asquith made an announcement which revealed his intention of shelving the Woman's Suffrage Bill. What followed is well known : the deputation led by Mrs. Pankhurst ; the sickening scenes round the House of Commons ; the coarse roughness of the police and of the hooligan element, encouraged by the police ; the orgie of brutality which has caused the name of Black Friday to be given to that day.

Emily was not amongst the many women arrested ; but the following day she broke glass to the value of £2 at the House of Commons, as a protest first and foremost against the treatment of her comrades on the previous afternoon, and secondarily as a protest against Mr. Asquith's conduct in regard to the Conciliation Bill. She was arrested, brought up for trial on the last day of November, and ordered to pay a fine of five pounds or to go to prison for a month. Emily, no more than her fellow-fighters, ever dreamed of paying fines, and once more she found herself in prison, this time in Holloway, where she was denied chapel and exercise and any means of communicating with her fellows. In protest against the treatment accorded to her she adopted the hunger strike, and after two days was taken to the punishment cells, where she again went through the tortures of forcible feeding until her release six days later. She was one of the seventeen prisoners welcomed at the Christmas lunch on the 23rd December.

Nineteen-hundred-and-eleven was the year of the Census, and large numbers of suffragists made it the occasion of a protest against their absence of political status by refusing to fill in the papers ; so large indeed were the numbers that the threatened prosecutions were of necessity abandoned. Emily's census paper contained these characteristic words : " As I am a woman and women do not count in the State, I refuse to be counted." Then followed her chosen motto : " Rebellion against tyrants is obedience to God."

Her method of avoiding the Census was to spend the night in the House of Commons, in Guy Fawkes' cupboard. Here she narrowly escaped the notice of an M.P. with two visitors, but being unable to get out of the crypt as the doors were locked, she was finally discovered by a cleaner. She was taken to Cannon Row Police Station, but, after being detained a few hours in the matron's room, was dismissed.

The desire to enter the House of Commons and to address its members was persistent : in June she was again arrested for being within its walls, " supposed for the purpose of committing a breach of the peace." The " breach of the peace," she informed the magistrate, consisted in an intention to address the House, and, there being no evidence to show that she intended to attack anybody, she was discharged, refusing, however, to give an undertaking not to return.

In December, 1911, she was again under arrest, this time for setting fire to pillar-boxes. Being discovered in the act of putting a piece of linen saturated with paraffin into one box, she confessed to attacks on others when charged at Bow Street, adding : " I did this entirely on my own responsibility."

Pending her trial she was released on bail, amused to find that she was thought worth a thousand pounds, which was the amount of bail fixed ; and she went to spend Christmas at Longhorsley. It was a happy time, the shadow of the coming trial notwithstanding; and one day of it was impressed with special clearness on the memories of both mother and daughter. Sunday, the 7th of January, 1912, was a day very clear and bright and calm; quiet, too, in the village, with fewer motors than usual passing by, few sounds of any kind outside. Within, by the fire, Emily sat and sang. Long ago at Gaston House she had sung ere she fell asleep ; later, to her father's accompaniment, she had sung with him; now, in her clear soprano voice, and with all the fervour of her militant heart, she sang the militant hymns she delighted in. Others, too, she sang: hymns like "Thy way, not mine, O Lord " ; hymns breathing forth an obedience of which, to Emily's way of thinking, rebellion against tyrants was an integral part. But it was the hymns of active endeavour that appealed to her most, and the one that her mother remembers best on that day is the one beginning " Fight the good fight with all thy might," for, as she sang it, Emily's whole soul seemed to be in her singing. Later on, writing to her mother from Holloway, she spoke of the happiness of that afternoon. On the day following it she went back to London to face her trial.

At that trial, on the 10th of January, 1912, she gave evidence of her quick wit and of that sense of fun which no hardships could drive out of her. Mr. and Mrs. Penn Gaskell accompanied her to the Court, where they found a large number of sympathisers waiting to go in, only to learn that all women were refused admission. In vain Mr. Penn Gaskell attempted to get the order for their exclusion refuted ; not a woman was to be allowed within. Close to the door Mrs. Penn Gaskell waited, hoping to catch a glimpse, to hear a word of what was going on ; and presently, to her amazement, she heard her name read out ; she was called as a witness for the defence. Quite coolly the prisoner began to put questions to the new witness, but questions so trivial that the judge put a stop to them. Emily's aim, however, was accomplished, an aim revealed to her friend by Emily's glance at her as she entered the witness-box. Mrs. Penn Gaskell was in the Court, and in the Court she remained till the end of the proceedings.

Emily was sentenced to six months' imprisonment, a sentence from which she appealed, but which was confirmed in the Court of Criminal Appeal.

It was in February that she entered Holloway, to pass through a time of suffering greater in length and intensity than any she had yet endured. Once again she experienced the horrors of forcible feeding ; this being practised upon her with every accompaniment of brutality and insult, not because she was pursuing the hunger strike, but because, her health and appetite having failed under prison conditions, the authorities considered that the food she was taking in the natural way was not sufficient to maintain her in health. In June she did adopt the hunger strike ; in June once again it seemed to her that the time had come where the giving of a life might save the lives of many others. And still the time was not yet ; not this summer, not this June.

The statement of what happened on June 19th, written by her after her release at the end of the month, is forcible in its vividness and simplicity :—

We were anxiously waiting the result of the Conspiracy Trial. Then the leaders demanded to be put in the first division. We waited for the result. The news came at last that a small

43

measure of justice had been won, and we lost the precious privilege of their presence. But at once we made our demand for similar treatment. We resolved, as usual, to give every opportunity for Constitutional pressure to win justice. For over a week we waited, every day asking for the Governor and demanding that we should be transferred to the first division, clearly warning him that if all other methods failed we should adopt the hunger-strike. The day before we did this we gave him a twenty-four hours' ultimatum, and then began our fight, strictly to time.

On Wednesday, June 19th, from 10 a.m. onwards, we were kept in solitary confinement.

On Saturday morning we decided that most of us would barricade our cells after they had been cleared out. At ten o'clock on the Saturday a regular siege took place in Holloway. On all sides one heard crowbars, blocks, and wedges being used; men battering on doors with all their might. The barricading was always followed by the sounds of human struggle, suppressed cries of the victims, groans, and other horrible sounds. These sounds came nearer and nearer in my direction. My turn came. I fought like a demon at my door, which was forced open with crowbars till at last enough room was made for one of the besiegers to get in. He pulled open the door, and in came wardresses and a doctor. I protested loudly that I would not be fed by the junior doctor, and tried to dart out into the passage; then I was seized by about five wardresses, bound into the chair, still protesting; and they accomplished their purpose. They threw me on my bed, and at once locked the door and went off to the next victim.

I lay like a log for some time. When I did recover a little, I got up and smashed out the

44

remaining panes of my window, then lay down again until I was able to get out into the corridor. In my mind was the thought that some desperate protest must be made to put a stop to the hideous torture which was now being our lot. Therefore, as soon as I got out I climbed on to the railing and threw myself out on to the wire-netting, a distance of between 20 and 30 feet. The idea in my mind was " one big tragedy may save many others "; but the netting prevented any severe injury. The wardress in charge ran forward in horror. She tried to get me off the netting and whistled for help. Three others came and tried their best to induce me to go into my cell. I refused.

After a time their suspicions were allayed, and the matron came through into the ward to visit some of the prisoners; while she was there the wardresses relaxed their watch, and I began to look again. I realised that my best means of carrying out my purpose was the iron staircase. When a good moment came, quite deliberately I walked upstairs and threw myself from the top, as I meant, on to the iron staircase. If I had been successful I should undoubtedly have been killed, as it was a clear drop of 30 to 40 feet. But I caught once more on the edge of the netting. A wardress ran to me, expostulating, and called on two of my comrades to try and stop me. As she spoke I realised that there was only one chance left, and that was to hurl myself with the greatest force I could summon from the netting on to the staircase, a drop of about 10 feet. I heard someone saying, " No surrender ! " and threw myself forward on my head with all my might. I know nothing more except a fearful thud on my head. When I recovered consciousness, it was to a sense of acute agony. Voices were buzzing around me; in the distance someone said, "Fetch the doctor." Someone tried to move me, and I called out, "Oh, don't!" Then the doctor came, and asked for me to be moved to a cell close by. They lifted me as gently as possible, but the agony was intense. It was all I could do to keep from screaming. And then I was placed on the cell bed. After a moment the doctor examined me, moving me as little as possible. He asked me to go to hospital, but I begged him to leave me there— which he did. I also managed to say, "For heaven's sake, don't feed me, because I shall fight." I was therefore left very quietly, and they brought me some water, and did all they could for me.

The first night was one of misery, as I had to lie on my back, although it hurt me to do so. There was no sleep. Next day I at once demanded that the Governor should allow me to have my own doctor to examine me. I said, "If you feed me before examination, it will be at your own risk." The Governor asked me why I had done my deed, and I told him I thought that one big tragedy would save the others. His hand trembled, and he promised that he would see into the matter.

I was left alone until about two o'clock, when a specialist came in with the prison doctors. He thoroughly examined me, and seemed very much struck with my injuries. Afterwards Dr. Sullivan confessed to me that he thought I had had the most extraordinary escape.

To my amazement, the doctors came to forcibly feed me that afternoon. The operation, throughout which I struggled, caused me such agony that I begged the three comrades who were released that afternoon to let friends know outside what was being done.

From that time on they fed me twice a day, in spite of the torture it caused me, until Thursday, when, to our intense relief, they fed us only once. We all said that any food that could have been poured into us in a second operation could not possibly have done us the good that the relief from a second torture did.

Meantime nothing was being done to make my condition better. My head was dressed on Sunday. Nothing further was done to it. By the examination I knew that besides the two injuries to my head the seventh cervicle vertebra was injured, and another at the base of the spine. They seemed very much worried about my right shoulder-blade. The sacrum bone was also injured, not to mention the many bruises all over my arms and back. All the vertebræ at the back of the head are very painful, and it is torture to turn.

On Thursday Dr. Sullivan examined me fairly carefully, and asked me to be weighed. I consented, and found that I had lost 4lbs. at least since the Friday when I threw myself over.

I may mention that when I went into Holloway I weighed 9st. 12½lb., and when released weighed 7st. 8½lb.

On the Thursday evening after the one forcible feeding operation, the doctor opened my cell door and announced the medical inspector. He walked in, and was followed by a gentleman who gave his name as Dr. Craig. The three of them sat down in my cell, and subjected me to a long examination and cross-examination. I calmly gave them all the information that I could, and seemed thoroughly to satisfy any doubts they had as to my sanity. In the course of the examination I believe I made them realise what a disgrace it was to England and the medical profession that such torture as forcible feeding should have been resorted to rather than granting justice to women. They weakly put forward the argument that their only mission was to save life, but could not deny that mental torture was hardly the safest way of doing so.

I also made them realise that we women set this great cause of ours before everything else in the world; or, as I put it to them, the cause of human progress was above that of any possible material consideration.

Dr. Craig thoroughly examined all my injuries, seemed greatly impressed by them, and when he shook hands with me said, "Don't do any more for your cause; you have done more than enough."

On the Friday morning, Dr. Sullivan examined me again, and told me that I should probably be released that day later on. He said he would not trouble me with the forcible feeding, if when I was released I would take some food before going out. I said, "Oh no; I absolutely refuse to take any food within the prison walls." He therefore decided that he must forcibly feed me again, for the ninth time —which was done.

All that day I got no chance of letting my comrades know that I should be released, which they would have been glad of, because they were all very anxious that I should be.

In the afternoon the doctor came and officially announced my release, said that all packing must be done for me, and asked me if, when I was in the cab, I would take some Brand's Essence. He said that the tin " should not be opened until I was outside, so that I should know it was not contaminated by the Home Secretary." I smiled and told him that I was willing to take anything once I was outside the walls.

" I smiled." The words are characteristic : she had the spirit but not the pose of the

48

martyr. Nothing ever broke her courage, nothing was able to keep for very long her sense of fun in abeyance or quite to destroy what Miss Hitchcock calls " the peculiar brightness of her look"; a brightness which, that same friend states, no photograph that she had ever seen was able to reproduce. But after this imprisonment she suffered much physically, and was laid up for a long time at the house of Mr. and Mrs. Penn Gaskell, where with the utmost care and tenderness she was nursed back to strength. At this time she spoke more than once of her idea that a life would have to be given before the vote was won, an idea which the trend of events and the action of the Government had deepened into a conviction.

"It may be so," Mrs. Penn Gaskell agreed, " but it is not your life that should be given. You have done enough—done your full share and more."

The answer was always the same, to this friend and to others : " Why not I as well as another ? "

To Emily Davison life was worthless save as it could be spent in the service of her cause. She knew now to the full what that cause stood for ; what it battled against, of miserable conditions, of the destruction of health and chastity and hope ; what it strove after, of purity and the power to remedy abuses. She who, as a schoolgirl, had been " easily moved by all that was noble and beautiful in literature and history," was moved now by life, and, hating oppression, put no limit to the price she was prepared to pay in her "rebellion against tyranny." Her readiness to sacrifice herself never wavered ; whether she was lying ill ; whether she was resting in Mrs. Penn Gaskell's garden—and one of her enjoyments was to spend an afternoon there, especially with the crowning delight of the cat upon her knee ; or whether she was at Longhorsley talking to the doctor or the priest, she was willing at any moment to risk or give her life.

Once with her mother, and once only, the matter was talked out, and then was no more mentioned between these two who were so close to each other and so dear. Indeed, during Emily's times at home it was arranged that the suffrage question should not be discussed ; her mother thinking it better that her holidays should be altogether holiday, and that in that house where were stored and treasured all the presents, no matter how trifling, that she had received from her childhood upwards, the outer life of struggle should be shut away and her thoughts turned to her other interests. "But she could not help talking about it," Mrs. Davison said, "and when the doctor came, or the Catholic priest, with whom she was friends, I would hear her in another room discussing it."

The doctor warned her that even her magnificent health and constitution would not bear the strain she was putting on them, but warnings of that kind fell on careless ears : she was to spend and be spent in the work she had been called to do.

Of all that she did during the last year of her life small mention can here be made. The tale of her deeds and endeavours, of her marvellous escapes, her daring and her courage, can only be fully told when the story of the Woman's Movement is enshrined in the annals of history. But all the time there was one who knew everything she did —the mother who awaited her coming. And when she came, this is the sort of conversation that would take place.

" Emily, what have you been doing ? "

" What do you mean ? "

" I have seen such and such a thing in the paper, and I know you were in it."

" But how can you ? When I am going to do anything, I always put you quite away from me, quite out of my mind."

" It's no good. I have a feeling always, on the day you do it, and then when the paper comes, I know which of the things was done by you."

In November Emily was in prison again, this time for assaulting a Baptist minister whom she mistook for Mr. Lloyd George. She was sentenced to ten days' imprisonment at Aberdeen, but was released after four days' hunger strike.

At this time she had no settled work, and consequently no salary, and employment by the Union was not compatible with the position of free lance which she had adopted. And yet, out of work, not knowing how she was going to live, and suffering from the effects of her long and painful imprisonment, her cheerfulness, according to the testimony of those about her, did not fail, nor her interest in subjects and questions outside the cause which was the inspiration and the chief object of her life. For she never lost that quality, compounded of many-sidedness and of absorption in the work or play of the moment which was so peculiarly hers ; the quality which caused her little French nephew and niece to be devoted to " Auntie Pem," who, while she took great interest in their studies, was able to join in their games and to enjoy cakes and chocolates ; the quality which, when staying with her sister at Dunkerque, caused her to throw herself heart and soul into all that was going on, thoroughly enjoying circus and fair, and impressing everybody by her liveliness and enthusiasm. It was the same everywhere she went and with everything she did. She was on the Executive of the Marylebone branch of the Workers' Educational Association, a federation of educational and work-people's organisations for bringing the higher education within the reach of the many, and her interest in the work of the Association was constant and profound.

Side by side with the interest she took in literature, in music, in the theatre, the stress went on ; all through the autumn and winter of 1912, all through the following spring. The time was not yet, but it was drawing very near.

In January, 1913, she was at Longhorsley. A letter written from there to an old friend shows that the simplicity of her school days lived in her yet.

BELOVED OLD SCHOOLFELLOW,

A happy New Year to you and yours ! I was indeed glad to get your card, and to find that you were still willing to " own me " ! I had not heard from you for so long that I had almost come to the conclusion that you, like many others, had got to the pitch of thinking I was *too* militant. . . . I am at present with my mother, who is glad to have me and to know that I am not too much battered. The long imprisonment last year, and the terrible finale, did not, of course, do me much good, but somehow I come up smiling. This last four days' hunger-strike in Aberdeen, of course, found out my weakness, and I have had some rheumatism in my neck and back, where I fell on that iron staircase. If it is wet or I am tired both parts ache, and I have bumps. My mother does not know this, thank goodness, and really, of course, I look and feel well. . . . At present I have no settled work here or in town. While here I busy myself writing my experiences and doing what I can to help my mother. . . . I wish I could hear of some (work) though.

53

This letter is signed with the old name, " Emelye," and before the signature comes a request for " a proper long letter soon."

Spring came with lengthening days. There were wild flowers in the hedgebanks, lambs were born in the meadows, and on great grassy stretches horses galloped in training for England's best-loved sport. And all the time the woman's war went on, and Emily was no laggard in the fight, taking in acts militant and non-militant, by speech, by pen, in word as well as in deed, her full share in that rebellion which to her was inseparable from religion, inasmuch as it meant obedience to God.

Spring drew towards summer. The season was in full swing, leading its votaries to crowded London gatherings, and out of London to the river and the racecourse ; and militant women were busy with preparations for a peaceful summer fête. It was nearly June, the month in which the fête was to take place.

On the last day of May, Emily, with Miss Clarke, the friend whose acquaintance she had first made when together they had received the Deputation contingents at the Great Central Station in 1908, attended a lecture given in connection with the Workers' Educational Association by Canon Masterman at the Bishopsgate Institute. She spoke on that occasion ; in the words of *The Highway*, the organ of the W.E.A., words written after her death, " she was urging the claims of the Association in the whole-hearted way so characteristic of her." "Hers was a sunny, cheerful nature," the paragraph goes on, " and in the W.E.A. it had full play. The stress of her life lay outside our limits, but with us she was happy as amongst friends. We are glad of it, and shall never forget her joyous presence."

After the lecture Miss Clarke suggested that they should go to tea at Toynbee Hall, but Emily did not fall in with the suggestion. On the following Saturday Canon Masterman was to give the fourth and last lecture of his series on City Guilds, and after the lecture there was to be a tea at Toynbee Hall and a presentation of books to the lecturer. Emily had already bought a ticket for this last lecture, and intended to be present at the presentation, and, " Oh no," she said, " we shall be going there next Saturday. Let us go and have tea and a chat somewhere quietly together."

So they went, the two friends, to the A.B.C. at the Holborn end of Southampton Row, had tea and sat chatting for two hours. Emily, her friend recounts, was in an expansive mood, disposed to talk, to linger, showing more affection than it was her fashion to display.

It was June, the month in which a year ago she had offered her body as a sacrifice, to be maimed or destroyed, in the hope of stilling the cries of pain about her. This June she was at liberty, free of prison walls, and able to go to " All in a Garden Fair," on the opening day, Tuesday, the 3rd of the month. The first thing she did was to take Mrs. Leigh to stand with her before the statue of Joan of Arc. Saluting, she stood there, reading the words upon the pedestal: " Fight on, and God will give the Victory." Prepared for battle Joan was figured, she who had heard voices and obeyed the Call ; in armour, ready to mount the charger which was to bear her in the fight for freedom and the honour of a king. On horseback or beneath horses' hoofs, what matter how the Call leads or where ? In the fight for liberty some must be always slain, and sometimes a king is sheltered and sometimes besought, and well it is if his honour be not smirched when the fighter falls.

Emily was never brighter than on that day. She stayed long at the Fair, and said she should come every day, "except to-morrow. I'm going to the Derby to-morrow."

" What are you going to do ? "

" Ah ! "

It was her usual answer, her head a little on one side, her eyes smiling, when she had planned something that she did not mean to divulge. " Look in the evening paper," she added, " and you will see something."

Derby Day. Packed trains and rushing

motors, and the rank and fashion of England and the scum and riff-raff all hastening towards Epsom Downs. A woman took a third-class ticket to Epsom ; a return ticket. Not fashionably clad this woman was, but in quiet, unnoticeable garments ; round her body, under her coat, was wound a flag ; another rolled tight was carried in her hand. Early that morning Emily had rushed into Headquarters. " I want two flags."

" What for ? "

" Ah ! "

" Perhaps I'd better not ask."

" No, don't ask me."

The crowds were great all the length of the course, and very close and dense at Tattenham Corner. Now it is the great race of the day ; fine horses, long watched and tended, carefully trained, are waiting for the start, with jockeys cool and keen and weirdly small ; and one horse and one jockey of great interest to the crowd ; the King's jockey, the King's horse.

They are coming ! Hark to the sound of them, and how the hoofs thud upon the turf ! There are women in the crowd ; one has a flag wound round her, hid by her jacket, and in her pocket the return half of a railway ticket. None notice her, or the other flag, held close to her side.

With a rush the horses come in a great swinging sweep round the curve of Tattenham Corner. There is a woman on the

57

course, there, in amongst the horses, and a flag waves, the colours of it purple, white, and green. A hand grasps at a bridle ; the King's horse swerves and falls ; the King's jockey is hurled to the ground ; cries and confusion everywhere ; one only heeds them not. For her there are no more sounds, of icy, rushing water, of comrades' cries, of prison voices. The life so often risked has been given ; the time has come.

At that same hour, in a house at Longhorsley, a woman stood in a room alone. She had risen that morning with a feeling that she knew, the feeling that always came when one far away from her was running into danger. And as she stood, something went by her—a bird it seemed. But how had it entered, how escaped ? for the window was shut and the door, and looking she saw that there was nothing in the room, no living thing, save only herself.

Emily's physical body lay for four days ere the physical life went out of it, but her consciousness left it, for even as she fell beneath horses' hoofs, at that same moment that " something " went with a flutter of wings through a room in her Northumberland home. " I never let myself think of you when I do things," she had told her mother. But her thought surely had gone to that mother as her soul drew back from life.

Many processions Emily Davison had been

in, but never one like this of the 14th June, 1913, when the marchers and the crowd were silent, and the face of the queen of it was hid. Close to where it started, a ragged man stood, holding a rose, ragged too, drooping, half faded, and as the coffin passed he threw the rose upon it. " Gawd bless 'er," he said. " 'E's bin waitin' this two hours to do that," said the woman beside him.

There were tears on the faces of many men, gibes on the lips of very few : silence was in all the street through which her body passed, half awe, half wonder. Midway for some of those who marched was a burst of sound; a dim church filled with the singing of women's voices ; not sad singing, but triumphant, almost glad. " Nearer my God to Thee," they sang, " E'en though it be a cross that raiseth me." And the words that might have been Emily's own : " Fight the good fight with all thy might ! "

Then through the streets again, through crowds, poorer, more ragged, denser. Women were in the crowds, with faces, some worn, some wicked, some hunger-stricken ; women for whom Emily had died. Most of them knew it not ; some never till now had seen " the suffragettes." Through these to King's Cross Station, whence the coffin was sent, " covered with most lovely flowers," as her father's had been in her description twenty years before, to Morpeth Church—" very old-fashioned, with a lich gate."

The writer first saw that church on an evening in July. A paved path leads through the lich gate edged with great squares of yew to the church's door ; and beyond the door the path goes on between borders of mown grass on which are clumps of rhododendrons, and behind them cedar pines and Irish yews. On the Sunday of Emily Davison's funeral the rhododendrons were in bloom.

The bloom had gone on the evening in July and twilight lay grey upon the many yews and cypresses and tall cedar pines that stand amidst the graves. But about the rail-enclosed burial place of the Davison family, sight has a wider field, and looking upwards—for the ground rises all the way from wall to wall of that graveyard—the sky was bright with the sunset, a brilliant red ; and looking downwards towards Morpeth very pale and clear, and hanging in the pallor, was a half-formed moon. Looking, the sight went on, beyond the churchyard into the width of the world, beyond the evening into the years ahead, and saw, from far away and from near, feet coming, many, many feet, treading the paved path through the lichgate till the stones were hollowed and worn ; the feet of pilgrims to the Church, " very old-fashioned," and on beyond it, upwards, to the grave of Emily Wilding Davison ; who died that other women might find it possible to live truer, happier lives ; who fought that other women might have freedom ; who gave herself to the Woman's Cause, without grudging and without fear, convinced, as every apostle of liberty has been convinced, that rebellion against tyranny is obedience to God, and never doubting that God will give the victory.

The Life, Times, Friends and Death
of Emily Davison

1
Introduction

'What every schoolgirl knows' about Emily Wilding Davison is that she was the suffragette who threw herself under the King's horse, who deliberately killed herself, who chose martyrdom for the 'Cause' so as to help gain 'Votes for Women' by bringing the suffragette cause to the attention of King, parliament and cabinet.

It was with this knowledge about the woman and her death that we started this book. This was what both of us *knew* about Emily Wilding Davison. What we both *felt* about it was that she must have been misguided, silly, a touch unbalanced. Certainly neither of us could imagine anything in present-day feminism that could make us contemplate such a thing, let alone actually do it. Emily, we both concluded at that stage, was a little over-the-top, and that explained her suicide. After all, we both felt, to martyr yourself for *the vote* was just plain stupid.

At the end of a long process of research, re-conceptualisation, thinking and writing, we have reached a very different conclusion. Now we know that Emily Wilding Davison certainly didn't 'commit suicide' or even 'choose martyrdom'; that she was a sensible and clever woman with a coherent political philosophy shared with many other sensible and clever feminist women; that comparatively few feminists at the time were interested in the vote as such; and that the greatest impact that militant feminism had – and indeed wanted – was not on the few hundred men who were 'law-makers' in London, but on the everyday lives of thousands upon thousands of feminist women throughout the country.

One of the major contributions that present-day feminism has made to knowledge is the idea that most of what counts as knowledge, as 'fact, the whole fact and nothing but the fact', is often partial or just plain wrong when it comes to things that concern women. 'Knowledge', feminist social scientists, historians, scientists and philosophers have demonstrated convincingly, is rather to be seen as a socio-political product, in a context in which most knowledge-producers are white middle-class 'first-world' men. This 'knowledge' emanates out of these men's view of what the 'facts' are. They see and understand from the position of their own social location (as we all do, of course), so their particular, partial view of things systematically misunderstands and misrepresents – in sometimes subtle but often in extraordinarily gross ways – the lives and experiences of women.

The history most of us have been taught is one-sided and the product of a specific world-view. However, it comes to us packaged as 'fact', as 'scientific' and 'objective'. One demonstration of this is the idea of colonialism promulgated in most first-world school curricula, certainly when both of us were at school.[1] The colonising process is seen as one in which explorers, administrators and soldiers pushed back the frontiers of savagery, imposing order and all the many benefits of civilisation on native peoples. But of course these explorers, administrators and soldiers were white; the aim of the process was economic gain and political dominion; its assumption was that 'white' and 'civilisation' were synonymous. It consequently failed to recognise complex and sophisticated but different civilisations even when these rebelliously smote it in the eye. One result of the process was that some sections of subjugated peoples accepted the colonisers' views of themselves as 'savages'; those who rebelled were ruthlessly suppressed, but what is more, their rebellion was discredited as the action of 'savages' opposing 'legitimate government' by their 'natural rulers'.[2] In fact, active opposition to colonialism existed from its very beginning. It is 'history' as it has been handed down to us that has hidden this opposition, or denied it.

Everything just said about the *racial* colonising process has been said equally legitimately by feminist academics about the *sexual* colonising process. In relation to history, women's lives and actions have been seen – and often not seen – by partial male eyes, which have defined what is 'proper' for women, and then explained away the rebellions of various categories of 'improper' women within an intellectual framework provided by the ideology of sexual colonialism. Such women, we have been told, were sick, bad, mad. Their activities could be, should be and were regulated, controlled, confined, and sometimes obliterated. When such women fought back, their activities were ruthlessly suppressed and the ideological apparatus of sexual colonialism discredited their actions, and indeed often their very persons.

This has been the fate of most feminists of the past who in various ways asserted women's rights and challenged 'male power' in open and vehement ways. Feminists, along with other groups of deviant women, are renegades – feminists, literally, *renege* on 'civilisation' as we are given it (Rich, 1983). This discrediting process has structured assessments of the activity of militant feminism in the Edwardian period until very recently indeed.

When we came to do our own research on Emily Wilding Davison we were to find that the woman, her philosophy, her actions and the movement of which she was a part were all not quite as 'history' had told us they were. We have worked on a wide variety of different kinds of evidence, including Emily Davison's own published letters, reviews and essays; her unpublished letters, notebooks and essays; contemporary newspapers; internal WSPU documents; newspapers and newsletters of the many suffragist – and anti-suffragist – organisations; memoirs and other autobiographical writings; present-day books, articles and newspaper reports. From our study of these we conclude that feminists bring a different 'eye' to historical evidence. We see it differently because different assumptions are made about it, and also different kinds of knowledge are brought to the work we do using it. We say this in general terms; it can also be said in the very specific circumstances of producing this biography.

One instance of 'seeing differently' the same evidence actually involves our understanding of what 'biography' is. Conventionally, biography involves a kind of intellectual spotlight trained on the 'famous dead'. The subjects of biography are almost invariably male – for unless she is a media star or courtesan or maybe a novelist, it is very difficult for a woman to be seen as 'famous' and thus a fit subject (or object) for biography. So to choose to study and write about a woman who does not have such public status is itself a seditious act.

During the last twenty years of this present feminist renaissance, feminists have emphasised over and over that 'stars' do not simply exist, they are created through a process which is *social, class-*

related and *sexual political*. Even the 'famous' started out as just a person among their peers. Einstein was just another spotty schoolboy, undergraduate, young working physicist, and other physicists shared many of the ideas we now think of as uniquely his. Simone de Beauvoir was just another bright middle-class girl, school-teacher, intellectual hanging round cafés talking politics and philosophy; other novelists, philosophers and political activists shared many of the same ideas, and other women developed equally stringent criticisms of the fate of the 'second sex'.

However, there are inestimably more 'Einsteins', in sport, literature and the arts, science, politics, exploration, religion and so on, than there are 'de Beauvoirs'. Women who might be famous if they were men remain *women* and therefore by definition secondary to the great and famous of their day. And, it is instructive to note, unlike her female peers, de Beauvoir lived and worked as an honorary male intellectual.

Moreover, the class position of all the Einsteins and de Beauvoirs that biographies are written about is by no means accidental. The daughters and sons of toil are apt to be seen (ah, but who does the 'seeing'?) as part of the 'herd'; and even significant figures in working-class history, such as Keir Hardie or Ellen Wilkinson, are much less written about and are deemed (ah, by whom?) less significant than many of their contemporaries: the Asquiths, Churchills, Beatrice Webbs, Countess Markieviczses, who just happen to be of a very different social and class background.

Our idea of 'feminist biography', then, is that it should look beyond the famous dead. It should eschew the 'spotlight on the famous dead woman' approach and instead locate the women who are its subjects within the social, political and intellectual context in which they lived and worked. One crucial part of this process is to recognise that people are social beings. Most people have parents, siblings and other family, and friends and lovers; but they also have what the women who figure largest in this book would call 'comrades'. That is, friends to whom they sometimes have passionate attachments but sometimes not, with whom they work politically, try out ideas, discuss work and talk about books, people, politics, ethics, life, death.

Our biography of Emily Wilding Davison locates the woman herself in a number of social and intellectual contexts. It looks at the basis of her ideas and actions and discusses her moral and political philosophy. It looks closely at Emily Davison's comrades, her closest friends, the women who provided each other with understanding, love and practical as well as intellectual support. It also tries to piece together militant feminism of the period, not at the level exhaustively discussed in most histories dealing with 'the suffragette movement' – the level of formal feminist organisations and groups and their dealings with governments and parliaments and elections – but instead at the level of informal networks and the understandings and states of consciousness which grew up in them.

Our idea of a feminist as distinct from any other kind of biography includes another departure from the canon of 'how to do it'. So-called 'modern biography' (Stanley, 1986) takes as its aim the collection of all the facts about its subject and out of these the construction of the 'real' X or A. It presents us with the final *product* of the biographical *process*. Readers are given something unseamed, unflawed, complete. However, a biography is only artfully thus: it has to be written into this form out of a much messier and certainly incomplete process of finding out and puzzling over. In practice, and as those of us who produce biographies know full well, only exceptionally do we experience final closure in relation to the person whose life and times we explore.[3]

Thus, in keeping with our feminist ideas about research processes more generally (Stanley and Wise, 1983; Stanley, 1988), we have eschewed presenting the reader with a 'final product', the biographic equivalent of a can of baked beans. Instead we have tried to write about the process of finding out about Emily Wilding Davison and all the many confusions, gaps and puzzles that this *still* involves. History and biography are much more interesting than historians and biographers let on. And a large part of their interest is that the process of doing them is so enjoyable but also so challenging. This challenge is both practical and intellectual. In order to find out, reduce the gaps, solve some of the puzzles, we had to go to libraries, order books and microfilms, thumb our way through countless notebooks, letters . . .

This is a very physical and indeed manual work process; but it is a manual process closely related to an intellectual one. We had to *think*: to assess 'the evidence' by assembling it into different patterns, to try to make connections, to look out for and see (sometimes without really knowing what it was that we were looking for) new evidence, new leads; and then to acknowledge when we failed or when the evidence so assembled pointed us in directions we didn't really want to go.

So far, 'we' has been used in describing some of the ideas in and assumptions behind the writing of this book. All jointly produced books involve some division of labour between the authors. The division of labour between us has been a singularly productive one, for it has enabled each of us to indulge ourselves in those bits of the research/writing process that we particularly enjoy.

Ann is most interested in finding out about 'the women themselves', in spending hours reading library catalogues to see what can be turned up, in going off to talk to any and everyone who might know something and in following up 'leads' opened up by this. Both of us like to sit in libraries reading through old newspapers and journals and to gossip endlessly to each other about what we have found out about the long-dead. Liz is most interested in the 'web of friendship' of feminist women of the past and how this relates to formal and informal feminist organisation, and most enjoys being surrounded by acres of old paper out of which a jigsaw puzzle of words can be pieced together and then spun on to a much smaller amount of new paper.

This is precisely how we have worked. The result has been that its product, the book you are now reading, has been written by Liz rather than by Ann. Of course we have discussed its contents, but such discussion is no substitute for saying something publicly in your own words, which is what Ann hasn't wanted to do. And so in what follows 'we' is used in relation to joint activities; otherwise either 'I' – meaning Liz – or 'Ann' is used. 'I', 'Ann' and 'we' appear a good deal in the pages that follow because the book really *is* a 'biographical detective story' and the story of what we/Ann/I did is told as much in the order of it happening as is possible. We found the process of finding out immensely exciting, as one thing followed or tumbled after another, and this seems the best way of conveying something of that excitement to you.

We take the idea of process very seriously. A book is merely a marker within a continuing process of finding out and understanding. As will become clear later, there are still aspects of Emily Davison's life and times that we understand only incompletely, assessments that we have made standing on rather thin ice, and some almost complete blanks. However, we hope that this book will interest, excite and infuriate our readers, so that you write c/o of

The Women's Press to tell us where we've got it wrong, and what else there is we should know. We hope that you do your own finding out and produce your own discussion and writing. At the very least we hope for help in solving some of the most infuriating gaps in what we know about . . .

Ah, but to name names, to say the biographical equivalent of the detective story's 'who dunnit', at this stage would never do! Read on.

2
Taking a View on Emily Wilding Davison

Picture the streets of London on Saturday 14 June 1913, ten days after Derby Day. Emily Davison has died. An inquest says 'misadventure', but the greater part of the feminist press says martyrdom. *The Suffragette* proclaims the glory in martyrdom and the absent Christabel produces grandly rolling sentences; *Votes For Women* more soberly notes all the details of the procession and then the funeral; and a certain feminist novelist and short-story writer provides material for *The Vote's* coverage of these sad events. These accounts note that from Victoria railway station to St George's church in Bloomsbury, where a service is held, to King's Cross railway station where the coffin is embarked for Newcastle and then Morpeth, the streets are packed with people.

Thousands upon thousands of people. Central London has come to a halt for this one dead woman. The crowds are mainly silent and respectful, though here and there some jeering voices demand, 'What about the horse?' and other remarks coarser than this. Through the silent streets silently walk some 6,000 suffragettes from all over Britain, most in white with black armbands, carrying flowers. At their head the tall, blonde Charlotte Marsh carries a cross with which, true militant comrade of Emily Davison and Mary Leigh, she beats a path through the occasional attempt to break up the march. There are banners, suffragette colours, Mrs Pankhurst's empty carriage, and the long, almost endless, stream of silent women. In their midst is a horse-drawn hearse, a purple-covered coffin with huge silver prisoners' arrows emblazoned upon it. Here too are some of Emily Davison's closest friends, and banners with her favourite mottos.

The next day in Morpeth there is a similar scene. Here are packed the most people Morpeth has ever seen in its streets. At least 30,000 people stand and over 300 suffragettes assemble as the coffin arrives and is placed on the hearse. The slow silent march from railway station to parish church begins. Then a small quiet family funeral, with Emily's mother, her aunt, her cousin, and her companion Miss Morrison, leading the way into the churchyard. The suffragettes silently wait. Later, they enter to pay their last tribute, many of them weeping, and the grave is piled high with flowers.

There are three main published sources of information about Emily Wilding Davison that are continually referenced in accounts of her death. In approximately chronological order these are: her entry in the *Suffrage Annual & Women's Who's Who* of 1913; *The Suffragette*'s June 1913 coverage of her death and funeral and the publication in June 1914 of her essay 'The price of liberty'; and Gertrude Colmore's biography. Although these sources each construct a view of Emily Wilding Davison in somewhat different ways, they are by and large complementary.

Emily's entry in the *Women's Who's Who* (written late 1912 or early 1913) is her own autobiography; it is reproduced as Appendix 1 (see pp. 186–7). This presents the public Emily, Emily the total militant, the woman whose life consists of various militant acts which culminate in arrest, imprisonment and forced feeding, but whose militancy is balanced by her literary interests and sporting proficiencies in swimming and cycling.

Here we see the militant as 'renaissance woman': the perfectly rounded human being who is scholarly, physically active, and completely dedicated to the 'Cause'. In assessing this portrait in miniature of Emily Davison it is necessary to keep in mind various things about the conditions of its production. It was produced at a particular juncture in Emily Davison's militant career, for a particular and public purpose; consequently it is likely not to have been the only view of herself that Emily had, the only autobiography that she constructed and presented to others.

We are all skilled biographers and autobiographers. Each of us constructs accounts of ourselves and our past histories to present to other people; and we construct and use similar accounts of other people too. We do this all the time: biography production and use is one of the main features of everyday conversation. However, what is perhaps unusual about Emily Davison's biography in the *Women's Who's Who* is that it consists almost entirely of (a) present-day rather than past events and (b) events of one kind: arrestable and punishable militant events. In a sense in this entry Emily Davison the militant, rather like Athene from the head of Zeus, springs into being fully fledged. Unlike for example the entry on Elsie Howey – which cites how she lived with her widowed mother, went to university and then to Germany, there discovered feminism, and became involved with the women's movement on her return to England – there is no 'before feminism' for Emily, nor even any 'before militancy'.

This can be explained largely by Emily Davison's position within the Women's Social and Political Union in late 1912/early 1913. By this stage, as Gertrude Colmore notes in a very low-key way (1913, p. 52), Emily's habit of acting on her own initiative meant that she was not in favour with the leadership of the WSPU, and indeed was seen by them rather as an unpredictable thorn in the flesh. Thus the Colmore biography can be seen as a legitimation of Emily Davison's particular interpretation of the militant career and a celebration of her role as a public figure – and private nuisance – within the suffragette movement.

Coverage of Emily Davison's death and funeral in *The Suffragette* of 13 and 20 June 1913 presents her as the dead militant martyr *par excellence*, a totally heroic figure whose life and death were the result of her total dedication to the feminist cause: both are seen in terms of sacrifice, a single-minded dedication of mind and body. This 'deliberate death, martyrdom for the cause' construction of Emily Davison's death following events at the 1913 Derby is given a greater emphasis by *The Suffragette*'s June 1914 publication of Emily's essay 'The price of liberty' (reprinted from the *Daily Sketch* of May 1914). The essay has become the lynchpin of latter-day writings which see her death as deliberately chosen for one particular grand purpose (achievement of 'the vote'). This has been partly because of its arguments concerning a 'perfect Amazon' who will sacrifice all 'even unto this last'; partly because of the tone of the language used at various stages in the essay, for by modern standards it is often 'purple' and 'over-the-top' (I discuss its content later).

If Emily Davison had not done anything bar wave a WSPU flag at the 1913 Derby, had lived on into a ripe old age giving taped interviews with sixties and seventies historians of the suffragette movement, little or nothing would have been made of 'The price of liberty': it would have been seen as a period piece in its use of grand but overblown phrases to convey fervour and passionate conviction. What allows it to be interpreted as, effectively, a 'suicide note' or a 'martyrdom note', is Emily Davison's death. However, to interpret it thus is to derive an ideological account of Emily's life from the facts of her death. Another example will help explain this point.

Dorothy Smith (1980) has analysed how the fact that Virginia Woolf chose to kill herself in 1941 has been used as a frame of reference in which to place, interpret and explain every other fact about her life and work. What permits this is an ideological construction known as 'suicide'. The term suicide is not a neutral one: it contains within it notions about (a) causes of suicide; (b) people whose personalities are such that they are potential suicides; (c) means of carrying out suicide. And suicide in this construction is most definitely seen as *pathological*, necessarily so, and thus requiring the services of specialist professional groups such as psychologists and psychiatrists. Thus various features of Virginia Woolf's life, such as her dislike of sex with men, her slightly malicious sense of humour, her liking for gossip, and also her feminism, are all interpreted and given meaning by reference to her suicide and indeed seen as contributory causal factors in that suicide. Dorothy Smith's paper also points up the fact that people used to 'kill themselves', but now it is very difficult to see this in any terms other than those provided by the ideology of 'suicide'.

'Martyrdom' was the explicatory frame placed on Emily Davison's 1913 death by her feminist contemporaries. However, and unlike them, latter-day interpreters of its meaning borrow largely from ideas about 'suicide', for this is the main version of 'killing oneself' that currently exists (men who kill themselves for political reasons, like the IRA hunger-strikers, are political martyrs; women who do so are treated very differently).

Gertrude Colmore's *The Life* was published at the end of 1913, some five months before the first publication of 'The price of liberty'. There is now no way of telling whether Colmore knew about this piece of Emily's writing and chose not to discuss it or whether she was not informed of its existence. It seems that the manuscript was in Emily Davison's papers. We think we have now established how it got from there into the hands of the *Daily Sketch*, who might have arranged this, and why it was thought necessary and appropriate – I discuss these matters in the chapter dealing with Emily Davison's closest friends. What can be concluded is that, no matter what 'the leaders' of the WSPU felt about Emily, once this essay had been published elsewhere, the powers that controlled *The Suffragette* would have felt obliged to reprint it.

Gertrude Colmore, too, presents a public Emily, 'Emily the total and dedicated militant'. But the way she does so, interleaved with more 'ordinary' features of Emily Davison's life, makes this a more substantial view of the woman than either of the two sources just mentioned, as well as a more enjoyably readable one.

Gertrude Colmore locates and explains Emily Davison's militant conviction and dedication mainly through the notion of 'genius'. This term is not applied *directly* to Emily Davison, but there is a strong indirect association of her with Emily Brontë, 'that other Emily, genius dowered', and they are seen to share a great individuality, a dedication, a single-mindedness of purpose, an iron will; and a complete conviction of the moral necessity for and sanction, not so much of their behaviours, as of 'themselves', their whole being as people of a particular kind. Readers cannot but note this conjunction of 'Emily Davison' and 'genius' and it informs our reading of what follows, for we are provided with example after example of behaviour or character traits exemplifying these qualities.

However, in the Colmore biography Emily's 'genius' is leavened by a host of human, endearing – but also, in contemporary terms, highly lauded – qualities. First and foremost there is the perfect relationship with her Mother (impossible not to use a capital letter here) and the sanctity and peace of her Longhorsley home. In our more cynical times it's difficult not to pull faces and doubt the perfection of this 'hymn singing by the fireside and winged soul leaving her mother at the time of her death', to dismiss this picture as so much sanctimonious hyperbole. Of course it could be a true picture, for sometimes daughters and mothers *do* have such perfectly enjoyable relationships with each other. There is also some discussion of the 'innately religious' Emily (Colmore, 1913, p. 19), the Emily who has an incredibly strong moral sense, who is concerned more with the heart of religion as applied morality than with the external shows of contemporary and male religiosity.

But there is also another Emily, an Emily who was a martinet with her siblings, and stubborn as a mule never was. An Emily who was a 'pickle', who was shy and endearing, worked hard and tried her best. This Emily liked musical comedy, was good at swimming and bathed late in November; she had a strong sense of humour and could laugh even in the midst of problems; even rarer, she could and did laugh at herself.

This is an ordinary everyday genius, as distinct from the extraordinary genius of the Brontës. It is an *achieved* genius, brought into being by will and decision and duty and responsibility. A quintessentially Victorian ideal of the 'self-help' and 'self-made' genius, it embodies an evangelical view of the feminist militant as a woman who sees morality in terms of putting its precepts into practice in everyday life and who takes on a dedicated responsibility for achieving the 'good life' through her own actions. This, then, is a style of feminism that has a good deal in common with English socialism – the socialism of Edward Carpenter and Eleanor Marx and other middle-class radicals who felt that socialism was to be gained only in the doing of it – and both share strong evangelical roots.

Nevertheless, Gertrude Colmore's *The Life* is still basically hagiography, even though it presents readers with a more rounded and more believable subject than *The Suffragette*. My conclusion is that it was *necessary* hagiography in feminist terms and I discuss my reasons for this in the final chapter. That she chose to present an entirely positive view of the woman in *The Life* underscores its completely political purpose and status. However, this has been consequential in terms of latter-day assessments of Emily Davison and her death.

We live in more cynical times in which hagiography is largely confined to a certain strain in biographies of film stars and politicians (and even these are usually counterbalanced by unauthorised, exposé writing). Froude's 'warts and all' biography of Carlyle and Lytton Strachey's 'beneath the surface' ironical look at eminent Victorians gave their contemporaries a severe shock, whereas today it is taken for granted as *the* way of doing biography.

Within *The Life*, as within *The Suffragette* coverage of the death and funeral, a finite amount of evidence is used to 'prove' the dedicated martyrdom, and no contrary facts, views or arguments are permitted to intrude. The modernistic trend in biography writing means that the conclusion drawn by Colmore from the limited evidence she presents – dedicated, perfect martyrdom – is subject to scrutiny, is ironicised, treated as hagiography. However, because so little primary source material has been used by later writers on Emily Davison, their assessments have been dependent on basically the same set of 'facts' used by Colmore, but a rather different conclusion has been drawn from them. Theirs is an approach which suspects and ironicises all 'perfect martyrs', which works in full awareness of ideas about 'suicide', and which also trades on more overtly sexist interpretations about women and women's behaviour. Thus major histories of the suffragette movement by Roger Fulford (1957), Andrew Rosen (1974) and David Mitchell (1977), albeit in slightly different ways, all treat Emily Davison's Derby act and consequent death as odd or peculiar.

In Roger Fulford's account, 'Davison, Emily' is absent from the index, while the account of her action and death is instead to be found under 'Derby, The'. In a largely respectful discussion, Fulford fails to locate her death in any sequence of events or any account of militant political philosophy, but rather states that 'she only typified . . . the consequence for a sensitive human nature of the brave deeds and loud words which poured forth from the militants'; he concludes that 'The foolishness of what she did is too obvious to need stressing' and that it was made neither better nor worse by 'the orgy of sentiment with which it was acclaimed' (Fulford, 1957, p. 286). This view seems to suggest that Emily Davison's action was merely passive: a sensitive nature was propelled by militant 'loud words' into 'obvious foolishness'; and it similarly fails to comprehend any of the surely political significance of the 'sentiment' that surrounded her death.

For Andrew Rosen, Emily Davison's Derby action does at least have a history, one located in her previous acts of militancy. However, Rosen uncritically accepts the Pankhurst view of Emily as an 'erratic', self-dramatising nuisance who was incapable of following official instructions, which is rather odd considering his generally negative assessment of the Pankhursts. He fails to consider that this view of her might be motivated and suspect or that her incapability could just as well be seen as a reasoned opposition shared with some other militant women. He sees her 1912 action in Holloway prison (when she tried three times to kill herself: I discuss this incident in detail on pp. 157–9) as 'seeking martyrdom', rather than accepting what she herself wrote about it: that it was an attempt to stop the mass forcible feeding that was happening around her that day. And his account concludes with an analysis of 'The price of liberty' that emphasises what in our times can be seen as 'sexual' language ('ejaculate', 'writhing' and 'consummation' figuring large in what he says).

David Mitchell notes that Emily Davison's 'incorrigible' freelance militancy was something she shared with other women, notably Mary Leigh and Charlotte Marsh. Indeed, his research is exemplary in its attention to detail and to previously untapped sources of evidence. But his political judgement is very conventional and his attitude to feminism and lesbianism is obviously one of threat and panic. David Mitchell portrays Emily Davison's Holloway action as merely 'unscripted drama' and sneers that, 'As Miss Davison had long suspected, she was worth more to the WSPU dead than alive' (Mitchell, 1977, p. 217). In addition, 'The price of liberty' is dismissed as 'bizarre' and seen as merely of a piece with Christabel Pankhurst's growing obsession with 'Male Lust'; its overtly expressed argument is simply ignored. In fact, as a careful perusal of *Votes For Women* and *The Suffragette* shows, this concern with 'Male Lust' was a long-established feminist bandwagon on which Christabel Pankhurst, out of sight and fast losing control of the most active and influential women in the WSPU, jumped fairly late in the day. I conclude that the 'growing obsession' is David Mitchell's, for he sees horrid lesbians everywhere in the WSPU: I picture him, poor man, writing while frequently glancing nervously over his shoulder and with one protective hand cupped over his crotch.

None of these accounts can be said to provide any rounded reassessment of Emily Wilding Davison's life or death. Rejecting the martyrdom frame of explanation, they see Emily's actions as incomprehensible and/or silly and/or foolish and/or the result of sexual repression and obsession. It is most instructive to compare these views with feminist accounts by contemporaries that are more detached than those provided by *The Suffragette* and by Gertrude Colmore – such as Rebecca West's (1913/1982), written in the thick of Emily Davison's death, and Sylvia Pankhurst's (1931), written after the passing of time.

For Rebecca West, Emily Davison was a sensible woman, one whom she had met, had seen collecting for socialist causes, whose death was in a sense forced by the petty stupidity of official reactions to women's just demands and would almost certainly be followed by that of Mrs Pankhurst. For Sylvia Pankhurst, Emily Davison was a woman of principle who used her own mind rather than mindlessly obeying 'leadership' dictates and who paid the price of that in terms of sneers about her character and behaviour; a woman who bravely protested against assaults and attacks on her comrades; and a woman who put her belief about the 'giving of a woman's life . . . to win the victory' (Pankhurst, 1931, p. 467) into practice. While interpreting her death differently, both women none the less take it absolutely seriously as a political statement by a sensible and brave woman.

This comparison reveals just how wide the gulf is between what the voices of recent historians say about Emily Davison's action and what the voices of contemporary feminists said about it. What lies in this gulf is time, like an ebbing and flowing sea, and a very different assessment of feminist philosophy, conventional politics and feminist friendships and communities. It is this complex contemporary assessment that I seek to reassemble in what follows.

3
Will the First Woman's Press Stand Up, Please

The wspu and the origins of the Woman's Press

We became seriously interested in trying to produce a reassessment of Emily Wilding Davison's life, times and death when Ann obtained a copy of Gertrude Colmore's *The Life*, published by the Woman's Press in London late in 1913. Even though *The Life* is a short book, we were impressed that it had been not only written but also published within six months of Emily Davison's death. We were also impressed by the fact that although the contents are hagiography, they are also *good* hagiography. That is, we have read many things written by many people about Emily Wilding Davison, but Colmore's biography remains a more complete as well as more accurate source of information about her than any more recently written account until this.[4]

Although we took full notice of the Colmore biography, both of us somehow completely failed to 'see', to recognise as something interesting, its *publisher*. We continued to pursue Emily Wilding Davison's life, friends, political involvements through many sources. However, a chance, fairly casual conversation with a friend (Candida Lacey of Pandora Press) about our work led her to express an interest in knowing more about the Woman's Press itself. Her interest sparked off my own and then Ann's; and soon the Woman's Press became a name that leapt off the pages of biographies and autobiographies and, most interesting of all, off the pages of contemporary feminist newspapers and in particular *Votes For Women* and *The Suffragette*.

The kinds of questions about the Woman's Press that needed to be answered concerned its origins, who had run it and with what aims, how its activities changed following its assimilation into WSPU headquarters in Lincoln's Inn in late 1912, how it operated after the assimilation, and under what circumstances it ceased operation. We also wanted to know why and how the Woman's Press had published Gertrude Colmore's *The Life*. We began to seek information which would enable us to answer at least some of these questions.

We first spotted the Woman's Press in early numbers of *The Suffragette* published in late 1912, where we saw a half-page notice that the Woman's Press had moved its offices into Lincoln's Inn House. *The Suffragette* was founded by the reigning inner circle of the WSPU after the 'split' with the Pethick-Lawrences in autumn 1912. This inner group was composed of Mrs Pankhurst, Christabel Pankhurst, Annie Kenney, Mabel Tuke, Flora Drummond, and others who moved in and out of the group from late 1912 to autumn 1914 when, effectively, the WSPU ceased to exist as a suffrage organisation. *The Suffragette* was published from November 1912, through its renaming as the patriotic and anti-German *The Britannia* in 1915, to its demise in 1918. As we read through every issue, we came to anticipate yet one more article under the name of Christabel Pankhurst, one more demonstration of the narrowing of *The Suffragette*'s focus from its mighty beginning to the last sad pages of *The Britannia*.

Late in 1913 a one-column anonymous review of *The Life of Emily Davison* appeared under the initials 'VSL' (*Votes For Women*, 19 December 1913, p. 225). We noted this with some cynicism, having become aware that the 'leadership' of the WSPU regarded the 'unpredictable' Emily with suspicion and, indeed, hostility. The length and anonymity of the review, and its location on one of the last pages of the 19 December 1913 issue, are of a piece with this. By this time, despite my initial reluctance, we had come to view Christabel Pankhurst with much disfavour (our feelings about Emmeline Pankhurst remain more complex).

Soon after this we began a systematic reading of *Votes For Women*. This newspaper was edited on behalf of the WSPU by Emmeline Pethick-Lawrence from October 1907, through the 'split' of late 1912 and a period of independence from any particular suffrage organisation, to the formation of the United Suffragist group in June 1914. Soon after this *Votes For Women* became its official newspaper (Pethick-Lawrence, 1938, p. 303). It ceased publication in 1918.

We saw with great interest *Votes For Women*'s continued expansion up to and for some time after the split in 1912. This expansion was not only of circulation and of 'coverage' in the narrow sense of the range of activities it reported, but also of 'breadth': links were drawn between women's oppression (not an inappropriate term to use for the kind of analysis developed in its pages) and the exploitation of the working class, the sexual and economic exploitation of children, and, although less well developed, racial oppression. The statement on the cover of all issues after the first few is one indication of this:

> To the brave women who to-day are fighting for freedom: to the noble women who all down the ages kept the flag flying and looked forward to this day without seeing it: to all women all over the world, of whatever race, or creed, or calling, whether they be with us or against us, we dedicate this paper.

Votes For Women's coverage continually emphasised that disenfranchisement was but one dimension of women's oppression. Indeed, the clear message is that 'the vote' was important as a symbol, or as 'the gateway'. It is important to note that the franchise (at least in their recorded pronouncements) was seen simply as an instrument or a tool even by those supposed monomaniacs on the subject of the all-importance of the vote, Christabel Pankhurst and Emmeline Pankhurst,[5] as well as by many other women, including Emily Wilding Davison.

The Freewoman, a feminist weekly, was published from November 1911 to October 1912. In numerous swingeing witty criticisms of the WSPU, its editor Dora Marsden (a former Manchester WSPU militant and an ex-organiser in Southport) emphasised over and over that behind 'votes for women' lay nothing but empty rhetorical mush. However, careful piecing together, aided by Rebecca West's later comments (published in *Time and Tide* in 1928 and reprinted in 1984), suggests that for 'the WSPU' one should read 'the leadership', in particular Christabel Pankhurst. I would argue that, faced by chapter and verse from *Votes For Women* and the clear statements in writing by various WSPU women such as Emily Davison, Dora Marsden's remarks do not hold up as a general critique, however much they may apply to the Pankhursts themselves (and I leave other people to argue this out).

The 'gateway' provided by women's enfranchisement would enable militant suffragist women to tackle a host of social ills by working together to change society from top to bottom. These ills included sweated labour, low pay, appalling medical provisions for childbirth, abominable housing, the framing of laws that resulted in the imprisonment of predominantly the poorest section of the working class only, and women's and children's sexual slavery. It is worth noting here that the analysis and programme of fundamental social change just outlined is to be found in Emily Wilding Davison's own writings, as well as in the sum of material appearing in *Votes For Women*.

In *The Freewoman* of 18 January and 14 March 1912 (pp. 172, 324) Dora Marsden insisted that the WSPU had no programme of political action and dismissed out of hand letters from individual suffragettes which pointed out in some detail what their personal political programmes were. Her remarks elsewhere in *The Freewoman* (27 June 1912, p. 104; 22 August 1912, pp. 263–4) concerning the bravery and incitefulness, if over-loyalty, of Emily Davison and Mary Leigh suggest that this criticism too must be seen as a product of her somewhat obsessional 'anti the (Christabelian) dictatorship' campaign.

It is worth noting that Dora Marsden's vehement criticisms of Pankhurst autocracy in *The Freewoman* were later seen as too sweeping by Rebecca West, who was on the staff of *The Freewoman* and later of the socialist *Clarion* and was herself no mean critic of the Pankhursts on other grounds (West, 1982). She suggested that the failure of the WFL as a mass feminist organisation (however active its democratically elected leaders were in London) pointed up the fact that Christabel and Mrs Pankhurst had read the political runes correctly. Many socialist-oriented WSPU women thought so too.

It has been claimed that the broadly based 'socialist' political philosophy we have discerned in the pages of *Votes For Women* and early issues of *The Suffragette* was actually associated only with Sylvia Pankhurst's East London Federation for Women's Suffrage and the 'militant suffragist' organisations of the north west.[6] This is a mythology comforting to those who believe that the suffragettes (i.e. members of the WSPU) were interested only in the vote for its own sake and only for middle-class women at that, and hence explains the demise of suffragette organisations once the vote for these women was won in 1918. However, such claims cannot be sustained by a close reading of the documents of the period. Later the writings of Emily Wilding Davison will be adduced in support of this argument. In addition, in Britain at least, any doubting reader can consult the three feminist papers referred to above (and others, such as *The Vote*, published from 1907 to 1937 as the newspaper of the Women's Freedom League; and *Common Cause*, the newspaper of the National Union of Women's Suffrage Societies, published from 1909 to 1913), reading not just the banner headlines and endless articles by 'the leadership', but the small reports of local events, lists of speakers, letters, all concerning women whose names are not well known but whose political histories can thus be traced through two, three and sometimes more feminist organisations of the period. Many public libraries in Britain have copies either in bound volumes or on microfilm, but those that do not can obtain them on inter-library loan – they make riveting reading.

The point about the broadly based aims of the wspu is stressed because the fact that some tens of thousands of women supported wide-scale social change (reform so wide-sweeping as to constitute a virtual revolution) provides a backdrop for Emily Wilding Davison's own ideas about social injustice and social change. A further important reason for emphasising these social aims relates to our growing discoveries about the original Woman's Press and its mushrooming of publishing activity.

The first Annual Report of the wspu, produced in February 1907, describes the large expansion achieved during the previous year. The number of full-time paid local organisers had increased from one to nine; the number of local branches had grown from three to fifty-eight; and financial incomings had leapt from nothing to around £3,000.

Charlotte Despard, Edith How-Martyn and Theresa Billington-Grieg, among others, left the autocratically governed wspu to found the more democratic – and, at a 'national' level, more overtly socialist[7] Women's Freedom League (wfl). The split came in September 1907 on the occasion of the first (and last) Annual Conference. Theresa Billington-Grieg had drafted a democratic constitution according to which wspu policy would be determined by a combination of local groups and representatives meeting at a regional level, and the annual conference itself. This was rejected by the rest of the leadership. Both Christabel and, probably more importantly, Emmeline Pankhurst produced strong and, for many WSPU members, convincing arguments in favour of 'Pankhurst autocracy' (although many others were puzzled or disturbed, or frankly disapproving, but remained in the WSPU and were quiescent on the issue so as to retain public solidarity and political effectiveness). The vote at the conference was clearly in favour of Pankhurst autocracy. A letter dated 9 September 1907 was sent by Mrs Pankhurst to all WSPU organisers and to anyone who wrote in or asked in person; while her speech at the conference itself was described by Mary Gawthorpe and Emmeline Pethick-Lawrence among many others as a powerfully moving *tour de force*.

It is interesting to note that there was never any pretence that democracy was the basis for WSPU action. Rather there was a straightforward claim that autocracy was legitimate in the specific circumstances; WSPU women were free to accept or reject it, but the leadership would retain control of the organisation itself, no matter what.[8] In spite of the surprisingly well-managed and largely friendly split between the WSPU and the WFL at the level of ordinary members,[9] by the time of the second Annual Report in February 1908 the WSPU had once more greatly expanded its activities and financial base.

Over the previous year the rooms occupied by the WSPU office at Clement's Inn had increased from three to thirteen and the office staff employed to run it had doubled. The number of subscribers to the organisation had tripled, while its annual income had somewhat more than doubled. This is an indication that the balance between the few independently well-off members who could donate large sums and the majority of less wealthy women had changed considerably; and of course it was to change still further in later years of the WSPU's life.

In the same twelve-month period, over 130 women had been arrested and/or imprisoned after militant activity following deputations, marches and processions held in connection with parliamentary failures to include women's suffrage in government policy. Five thousand meetings had been held all over Britain. One example of the expansion of activity in this period is that under the aegis of a particularly enthusiastic organiser, Helen Fraser, the WSPU began to be very active in Scotland, setting up its own separate office and staff in Glasgow in 1908 (see *The Suffragette*, 14 May 1908), with branches in Glasgow, Edinburgh, Dundee and Aberdeen. The number of Irish feminist groups also began to grow and become more militant.[10] By 1913 there were thirty-two women's and four men's suffrage organisations in Britain and eight women's suffrage organisations in Ireland (*Suffrage Annual & Women's Who's Who*, 1913).

From February 1907 to February 1908, over 100,000 publications had been sold by the WSPU and had raised an income of £750. We later found that by the summer of 1908 the WSPU literature department had been reconstituted as a self-managing 'Woman's Press department' under the management of a full-time worker, Mrs Knight (VFW, 3 September 1908, p. 430), selling not only penny pamphlets and other propaganda and discussion literature but also a range of items for use at the June 1908 mass meeting in support of women's suffrage organised by the WSPU in Hyde Park.[11] By autumn 1908 (when a large advertisement appeared in *Votes For Women*) the Woman's Press was selling a wide range of products.

As Fred Pethick-Lawrence noted in the *Votes For Women* of 15 September 1911 (p. 793), his offer in 1908 to run the literature department 'on a trade basis' and with quite separate accounts had been accepted by its ruling committee. The importance of selling propaganda had been learned from socialists like Robert Blatchford (his *Merrie England* had sold many hundreds of thousands) as well as from feminist precursors such as Annie Besant, whose birth-control publications and the overtly feminist *The Political Status of Women* (1874) had been hugely successful (Museum of London 50.82/97). To control propaganda gives a potential for a wider power position and for organisational control itself. In fact until the split in autumn 1912 and the banishment of the Pethick-Lawrences, the Woman's Press was run in close cooperation with the rest of the WSPU. However, the conditions of its organisation from 1908 meant that it could have become an entirely autonomous power base.

The products sold by the Woman's Press included a list of some twenty penny pamphlets;[12] a range of books, some of which were imports; postcard portraits of the leading figures in the WSPU[13] – there were in 1908 postcards on sale of the two Pankhursts, Emmeline Pethick-Lawrence, Annie Kenney, Flora Drummond, Mabel Tuke and Mary Clarke (Emmeline Pankhurst's sister, who died following assault on Black Friday, 18 November 1910); badges, ribbons, scarves, ties and belts with WSPU emblems and colours; and regalia in WSPU colours for use in processions and marches.

This latter item was no frippery. In addition to the great Hyde Park meeting, at this time the WSPU organised frequent marches through the streets not only of London but also of the many other towns and cities where local WSPU groups were active. These were an essential part of its political programme and an important means of recruitment to WSPU membership. In December 1908 the Woman's Press was also advertising a calendar and Christmas cards; later additions to its stock included a bag in WSPU colours and both tea and coffee in suitably emblazoned containers.

By the publication of the third Annual Report in February 1909, WSPU income had once more increased greatly, paid office staff had increased to seventy-five, while some hundreds of women worked at various times as volunteers, and nineteen rooms were occupied at Clement's Inn. The circulation of *Votes For Women* had increased to nearly 30,000. The number of branches and of paid organisers, of meetings held, protests made, women arrested and imprisoned, had all increased greatly once more. The Woman's Press department was firmly established, with an income of around £2,000 for the previous 12 months: and as well as selling its other products, it had sold a full special edition of *Women and Economics* by Charlotte Perkins Stetson (later Charlotte Perkins Gillman).

Independence at Charing Cross Road

On 6 May 1910 *Votes For Women* (p. 514) carried a report of the opening of the Woman's Press offices and shop at 156 Charing Cross Road in central London by Fanny Brough and Evelyn Sharp. We have been able to find out little about Fanny Brough other than that she was first arrested in April 1909 (VFW 2 April 1909, p. 507), played Lady Proudfoot at the Royalty Theatre not long after this (VFW 21 May 1909, p. 690) and was an active member of the Actresses' Franchise League. In contrast, much more is known about Evelyn Sharp (her papers are to be found in the Bodleian Library in Oxford).

Evelyn Sharp was a militant member of the WSPU, an active member of the Women Writers' Suffrage League (WWSL), and also was recruited by Emmeline Pethick-Lawrence to help run *Votes For Women* in March 1912 (*Suffrage Annual & Women's Who's Who*, 1913; Pethick-Lawrence, 1938, p. 264).[14] Later, with the Pethick-Lawrences, she became involved in the United Suffragists. She was also a paid WSPU organiser in various places, including Kensington in London.

We later found that the Woman's Press had become an even more important part of WSPU organisation by 1910.

At some point between February 1909 and May 1910 the Woman's Press office on Charing Cross Road had taken over the publication of *Votes For Women*. Although editorial control still remained with the Clement's Inn staff under Emmeline Pethick-Lawrence and Evelyn Sharp, distribution was organised from 156 Charing Cross Road. These 'spacious' premises consisted of eleven rooms on a number of floors previously occupied by 'the bookseller, George Allen' (VFW 10 May 1910, p. 514). The shop front attracted buyers and offered scope for publicity – a WSPU 'Votes For Women' clock on the building was a very visible symbol of feminist presence in the area.

The 1 July 1910 edition of *Votes For Women* (p. 651) provided us with a graphic picture of life at 156 Charing Cross Road. Following the June 1910 Hyde Park demonstration, callers streamed into the shop searching for information about the militant struggle of the WSPU, looking for books, pamphlets and leaflets about numerous aspects of national and international feminism and other radical movements; and of course sometimes simply searching for other like-minded women, other feminists. By this time Mrs Knight was in charge of a staff who, in the six rooms over the shop, organised the weekly distribution of *Votes For Women*, produced posters advertising meetings, and sent out orders of badges, belts, ties, tea ('both China and Ceylon'). It is clear that by this time 'propaganda' was very important indeed. But it is *Votes For Women* of 15 September 1911 (pp. 792–3) that provides the most interesting look at life in the Woman's Press offices, for one whole page contains photographs.

The visible source of the Press's growth and move was Emmeline Pethick-Lawrence, editor of *Votes For Women*. However, behind her was the *éminence grise* of the WSPU, Frederick Pethick-Lawrence.[15] Much of the necessary money and a good deal of the day-to-day organisational expertise which underlay WSPU growth seemingly came from 'the Pethick-Lawrences'; and it is now very difficult to disentangle what came from which of them, or indeed just how important either actually was to the growth of the organisation. Various previous accounts have suggested that the greatest input came from Fred; this seems an overgeneralisation and oversimplification of the multiple events and changes of a six-year period involving a complex relationship between two powerful people and an equally complex organisation containing other very powerful people.

Our reading of *Votes For Women* convinced us that even in 1910 the rest of 'the leadership' was apt to underplay the importance of day-to-day low-key organisational work in maintaining a constantly active militant edifice. This tendency became progressively – or, rather, regressively – more extreme after women like Dora Marsden and Mary Gawthorpe (who jointly edited *The Freewoman* in its early days) and many others who rejected wspu autocracy or policy or both left the organisation in 1911. This was followed by the expulsion of first the Pethick-Lawrences and then Sylvia Pankhurst and the East London Federation for Women's Suffrage in late 1912 and late 1913/early 1914 respectively.

We concluded that of the wspu 'names' the Pethick-Lawrences and Sylvia Pankhurst remained most committed to the importance of constant processions, marches and mass meetings, not only for overt propaganda purposes but also for membership recruitment. From 1910 until the 'Peth and Pank split' in late 1912, the Woman's Press continued to grow, as shown by the content of its frequent advertisements in *Votes For Women*. The list of books it published and/or distributed continued to expand, and contained some very distinguished titles indeed. Just a few weeks after the Pankhurst take-over, the Woman's Press advertised the following titles in *The Suffragette* (22 November 1912 p. 88):

Articles of Faith in the Freedom of Women L. Houseman
For And Against Lady Sybil Smith
Lady Geraldine's Speech (a play) Beatrice Harraden
Lysistrata Lawrence Houseman
Marriage as a Trade Cicely Hamilton
Marriage and Divorce Cecil Chapman
Mary Wollstonecraft G.R. Stirling Taylor
No Votes, Votes for Women Lady Constance Lytton

Press Cuttings Bernard Shaw
Public Speaking and Chairmanship G.E. O'Dell
Record of Women's Suffrage Helen Blackburn
Suffragette Sally G. Colmore
The Awakening of Women Frances Swiney
The Prisoner (an experience of forcible feeding)
The Servant Problem
The Subjection of Women John Stuart Mill
The Sphere of Man Mrs C.C. Stopes
The Suffragette Sylvia Pankhurst
The White Slave Trade
Under the Surface I. Martindale
Votes for Women (play) Elizabeth Robins
Why? Elizabeth Robins
Woman and Labour Olive Schreiner
Women's Secret Elizabeth Robins
Woman's Suffrage Arnold H. Mathew
Women's Fight for the Vote F.W. Pethick-Lawrence
Women and Economics Charlotte Perkins Gillman
Working Women and Divorce

The names of authors and the order of books are given just as they appeared in the advertisement (and appearing above the ad. is a short story by Gertrude Colmore herself), but it's worth emphasising some of these names. Laurence Housman was a very distinguished playwright and an active member of the Men's League for Women's Suffrage. Cicely Hamilton's *Marriage as a Trade*, Olive Schreiner's *Woman and Labour* and Charlotte Perkins Gillman's *Women and Economics* are all now recognised as important analytic works of Edwardian feminism, while Elizabeth Robins' *Votes for Women* is perhaps now best known as a forerunner of her extremely influential novel *The Convert*. Helen Blackburn's book is a now classic history of British feminism from the 1860s on. By no means least in this list is Gertrude Colmore's *Suffragette Sally*, published by Stanley Paul in 1911 (and reprinted in 1986 by Pandora Press as *The Suffragettes*). This and the publication of her 'Sketches' by *Votes For Women* establishes her connection with the Woman's Press before the writing and publication of *The Life of Emily Davison* in 1913.

After the Pethick-Lawrences were expelled from the wSPU, they retained *Votes For Women* whereas the Woman's Press itself was re-absorbed into the WSPU. On reading the biographies of Emmeline and Fred Pethick-Lawrence (1938; 1943), I was interested to find that neither contains any discussion of the fate of the Woman's Press. I conclude that the Pankhurst leadership knew that the WSPU had to have an 'official organ', to use the organisational jargon of the day; although the WSPU majority had editorial control, they needed the Woman's Press to produce the new newspaper, *The Suffragette*, quickly and with the minimum of organisational change. Always efficiently ruthless where 'the necessary' was concerned, it seems likely that the Pankhurst leadership 'allowed' the still discretely loyal Pethick-Lawrences to keep *Votes For Women* but retained for themselves all the apparatus of its production and distribution: the Woman's Press.

This is plausible conjecture. What is certain is that by early November 1912 the Woman's Press had vacated the Charing Cross Road premises and had moved into WSPU headquarters in Lincoln's Inn House. We still have not ascertained why, although strong clues exist: the Pankhurst leadership was partly *in absentia*, for Christabel Pankhurst, in retreat from arrest and forcible feeding, lived in Paris from March 1912 until war broke out in August 1914. This, coupled with the well-known aversion of Mrs Pankhurst to anything that smacked of office work, resulted in first Annie Kenney and then Grace Roe acting as Christabel's lieutenant-in-charge at Lincoln's Inn. A separate Woman's Press with its own premises and manager would have offered a very useful power base to any future challenger to the Pankhurst leadership of the WSPU, so perhaps it seemed safer to bring the Press as close as possible to Christabelian authority.

The Woman's Press and the Colmore biography

Since we cannot discuss the Woman's Press' publication of the Gertrude Colmore biography of Emily Wilding Davison with the protagonists, and they have left no letters about it, a puzzle remains. It was common knowledge at the time that the WSPU leadership did not favour Emily Davison. Her behaviour was seen as unpredictable, which meant that she had a nasty habit of initiating militant action which other women then followed and which thus remained beyond leadership control. There are two good indications of their disapproval. One is the general failure to highlight or praise Emily's militant activities after the 'Peth and Pank split', even when they were noteworthy – a comparison of the pages of *The Suffragette* and those of *Votes For Women* in this period shows this clearly. The other is that even when her activities were considered in any detail, as when Emmeline Pankhurst describes her setting fire to the three letter boxes in December 1912 in *My Own Story* (1914), the account is misleading and omits some key facts (a point I return to).

In spite of this disapproval, it is by no means surprising to find Emily's death and funeral reported as heavily as they were in the pages of *The Suffragette*. Christabel wrote discursively on it, as a 'martyr's death' pure and simple: Emily sacrificed herself for the cause, to help gain votes for women. Indeed, the fact that her death could plausibly be presented in this way made it far too good an opportunity to be missed. Hence the discussion and the reporting, and, at least in part, Grace Roe's organisation of the magnificently over-the-top funeral procession in London and, through the Newcastle WSPU, the procession in Morpeth itself.

However, it then becomes difficult to understand why Christabel Pankhurst's panegyric on Emily's death and funeral in June 1913 was not followed through to an equally eulogistic review of Gertrude Colmore's *The Life* on publication in December 1913. It certainly *wasn't* followed through: it would have been easy to have missed the December review, tucked away on a back page of the paper, only one column long (there were three to a page), appearing under the anonymous initials 'VSL'. This is in stark contrast to the reviewing of Constance Lytton's *Prisons and Prisoners* (1914). Con Lytton was in her own way another martyr to the cause: she had had a heart attack and then a stroke as a delayed consequence of having been forcibly fed as 'plain Jane Warton' (see her own account of this in *Prisons and Prisoners* and her full understanding of the role of class oppression and class differentiation with regard to Edwardian prison populations). The failure of the prison authorities to detect 'heart disease' in ordinary Jane Warton where they had been so swift to detect it in Lady Constance, sister of Lord Lytton and daughter of an Earl who was a former British Viceroy of India, and her resulting incapacity had been fully reported in *Votes For Women* (28 Jan 1910, pp. 276, 280; 4 Feb 1910, pp. 292, 298; 18 Feb 1910, p. 321; 22 April 1910 p. 479). The coverage of Con Lytton's book was consistent with this: there was over a full page review by Christabel Pankhurst herself in *The Suffragette* of 13 March 1914 (pp. 485, 497) and another full page review in the next issue (20 March 1914, p. 509). *The Suffragette* reprinted a review under the heading 'Two Great Books': *Prisons and Prisoners* and Christabel's *The Great Scourge And How To End It* (8 May 1914, p. 83).

Of relevance to solving the puzzle of the discrepancy between the voluminous coverage of the funeral and the minimal coverage of Colmore's *The Life* is the interesting fact that the wspu headquarters were run by Grace Roe from 30 April 1913 until 23 May 1914, when she was arrested for conspiracy, imprisoned, forcibly fed and heavily drugged by the prison authorities (*The Suffragette*, 12 June 1914, p. 160). In an interview with Antonia Raeburn (1973, pp. 193–8), Grace Roe talked about how she came to take on the responsibility of running the office and producing *The Suffragette* after the arrests of Annie Kenney, Miss Kerr and Mrs Saunders for conspiracy in April 1913. In a lull between frantically arranging finances, planning a trip to Paris to see Christabel, avoiding her own possible arrest, and trying to put together an issue of the paper from the remnants of copy which workers had managed to keep back from the police trawl, she sat in a daze. She then heard a voice say, 'Shall we win?' '"Yes," I answered, hardly recognising my own voice. "Thank God!" said the friend at my side.' (Raeburn, 1973, p. 195). The friend at her side in the wspu office was Emily Wilding Davison. Christabel Pankhurst might have spent an hour or two writing a panegyric for the dead Emily, but Grace Roe must have worked many hours every day from 8 June to 15 June to organise the truly amazing funeral for her dead friend. Part of this might have been for 'the cause', but surely a large part of it was for a dead comrade whose death she must have mourned with sad fury.

Again a conjecture, but it seems possible that it might have been Grace Roe who arranged the Woman's Press publication of the Colmore biography. Grace Roe knew several of Emily's close friends, including Rose Lamartine Yates. Rose was also a friend of Mrs Harold Baillie-Weaver – otherwise known as Gertrude Colmore. If this is so, it leaves another puzzle to solve. If Grace Roe had enough authority to arrange the Woman's Press' publication of the Colmore biography, then why couldn't she ensure that the review of the book was much more in keeping with *The Suffragette*'s coverage of Emily's death and funeral? So far we have been unable to find out.

Grace Roe was arrested at the end of May 1914. Until the start of the First World War she remained in prison and the wspu office was run by another 'understudy', who remained unnamed to help her avoid being rounded up and arrested like her predecessors. Following the outbreak of war the Pankhurst leadership called for an immediate end to militancy[16] and soon after this all wspu, wfl and Men's Union for Women's Enfranchisement prisoners were released. *The Suffragette*, renamed *The Britannia*, became less a feminist journal, more a means of instilling not only patriotic support of the war but also a militant anti-German fervour among erstwhile suffragettes.

However, the Pankhurst leadership – like Millicent Garrett Fawcett of the National Union of Women's Suffrage Societies (nuwss) in a somewhat different way – badly misjudged the likely reactions of many wspu ordinary members to the war. They miscalculated the ease with which militancy on the question of women's rights could be translated into militancy in support of war and 'patriotism' for the majority of wspu members. This point is discussed later; its relevance here is that the misjudgement brought about the premature death of the wspu, *The Suffragette* and the Woman's Press. That their demise was by no means inevitable is demonstrated by a number of factors. One is the 1914 rise of the United Suffragists, in which the Pethick-Lawrences became involved, and its continuance throughout the war. Another is the survival of militant suffragism in another guise, that of active pacifism. To speak of feminist pacifism as the continuance of feminist militancy might seem paradoxical, but in practice they seem to have been to a great extent synonymous.

4
Desperately Seeking . . . Gertrude, Mary, Elsie, Vera, Edith, Elinor, Rose – and 'A Loving Aberdeen Friend'

Of Gertrude and others

I was convinced that the best way of finding out more about Emily Wilding Davison the woman, as distinct from both Colmore's hagiographical legend and the latter-day mythology of a mindless suicidal fanatic, was through discovering more about the company she kept: her closest friends and associates. By locating Emily within a web of friendship and comradeship I felt we would find out inestimably more about her than we would through any other means. It also seemed likely that Gertrude Colmore would connect with Emily's circle of friends and associates, considering the circumstances of the book's swift production and publication by the Woman's Press. Given that our almost complete lack of information about Gertrude Colmore was driving Ann crazy with curiosity, we began the search for Emily's friends with her.

Of Gertrude Colmore's books perhaps the best known in her lifetime was *Suffragette Sally*, published by Stanley Paul in 1911 and distributed by the Woman's Press. The recent Pandora Press reprint as *The Suffragettes* (1986), edited by Dale Spender, contained some tantalisingly brief remarks about Gertrude: she sometimes published as George Colmore, her novel contained barely disguised portraits of well-known suffragettes, she wrote other novels.

After a visit to Manchester Central Reference Library and a

THE LATE MISS E.W. DAVISON.

Emily Wilding Davison's degree award photograph, used on the
WSPU 'In memorium' leaflet prepared for her funeral
(Mary Evans Picture Library).

**Mary Leigh's release from prison parade, 1908
(Fawcett Library).**

ABOVE LEFT: **Part of Emily Davison's funeral parade;
a banner with one of her favourite mottos, accompanied by
May Billinghurst and 'Miss Paynter'.**

BELOW LEFT: **The Davison home in Morpeth before Charles
Davison's death, now used by the Freemasons.**

Edith Mansell-Moullin (Museum of London)

ABOVE RIGHT: Edith Morrison; on the back a Claverton WI member has noted 'Miss Morrison, not as we knew her but the only one her brother thought suitable'.

Edith Mansell-Moullin (Museum of London).

BELOW RIGHT: Emmeline Pethick-Lawrence (Mary Evans Picture Library).

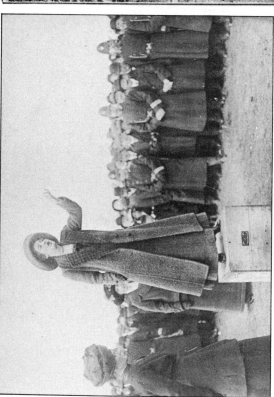

Rose Lamartine Yates speaking on Wimbledon Common (Museum of London).

RIGHT: The Woman's Press offices and shop front on Charing Cross Road, from *Votes for Women*.

Derby Day, 1913: Emily Davison has just been hit by the King's horse Anmer.

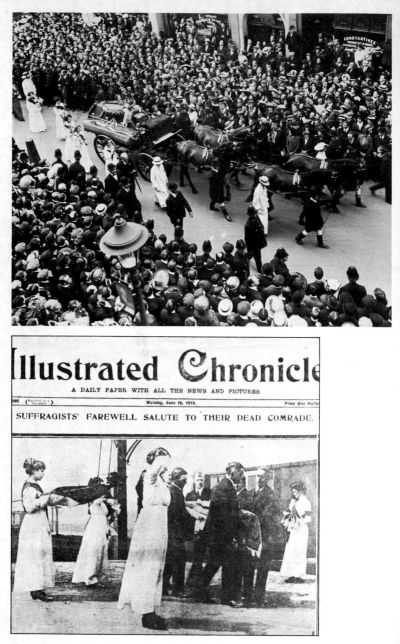

ABOVE: Emily Davison's funeral parade in London.

BELOW: Emily Davison's coffin being removed from the train at Morpeth.

browse through the British Library catalogue, we had a complete list of everything Gertrude Colmore wrote (or so we thought at the time); the British Library catalogue entry is reproduced as Appendix 2 (see p. 188). However, simply knowing what books she wrote took us very little further towards the woman herself nor gave any clue as to how and why she became Emily Wilding Davison's biographer. Our search continued via book reviews in *The Times Literary Supplement* (TLS), and obituaries.

The TLS provided us with reviews of four of Gertrude Colmore's novels, *The Crimson Gate* (30 June 1910), *A Ladder of Tears* (6 May 1914), *The Guardian* (11 January 1923), and her last book, *A Brother of the Shadow* (6 January 1926). Relying on reviews as a guide to style, content and approach is hazardous but often necessary given the problems of obtaining copies of women's literature from this period and before. It proved necessary in Gertrude Colmore's case. With this caution in mind, it seems that Gertrude was willing to tackle 'difficult' social themes as a novelist, themes in keeping with contemporary feminist concerns: illegitimacy; the relationship between sisters; a recognition of the importance of everyday life; the evil use of power, including 'spiritual' and religious power, by some men.

Interestingly, according to its reviewer, *A Ladder of Tears* takes the form of a fictional 'imaginative biography'. Moreover it adopts what Olive Schreiner called 'the method of life' in the foreword to *The Story of an African Farm* (1885). Life, as distinct from art, was for Schreiner essentially untidy and unpredictable. With echoes of this, the TLS reviewer describes *A Ladder of Tears* as 'a thing not of manufacture but of growth', which 'gives you the impression that its author Mrs G. Colmore was not making but watching and interpreting' (TLS. p. 140).

From the British Library catalogue we knew that Gertrude Colmore was a pen-name, that she had started out as Gertrude Renton and was afterwards Dunn and then Weaver. Ann's search for obituaries focused on the names 'Gertrude Colmore' and 'Gertrude Weaver' and on the year 1926 (the review of *A Brother of the Shadow* noted that the author died that year). *The Times* gave us obituaries for Gertrude Baillie-Weaver (27 November 1926, p. 14) and for Harold Baillie-Weaver (20 March 1926, p. 13): her husband, we deduced from the contents. In the *Manchester Guardian* of 29 November 1926 (p. 14) Ann found another obituary for Gertrude, while *The Times* of 9 January 1927 (p. 17) provided some details about her will. We sat back to digest these.

Gertrude Renton died in Wimbledon but had lived previously in Widdington near Newport in Essex, and was cremated in Golders Green. She was the sixth daughter, went to school in Frankfurt, was taught privately in Paris and London and was first married to H.A. Colmore-Dunn, a barrister with an interest in fencing. More importantly, perhaps, in 1901 she married Harold Baillie-Weaver, also a barrister. With him she shared not only an involvement with the Theosophical Society (some of her views on which are contained in her last novel) but also the cause of animal rights; she and Harold were joint founders of the National Council for Animals' Welfare Work. She is said to have been 'fragile and delicate' and to have had a 'gentle, refined personality', but she was also physically and morally courageous and hard-working in causes she took up. These, *The Times* correspondent notes, included not only the non-militant but also the militant suffragist cause and pacifism: the latter involved her being stoned in Saffron Walden in 1914 when she spoke against the coming war. Some of Gertrude Colmore's political concerns were confirmed by her will, in which she left money to a range of animal rights organisations and to the Theosophical Society. When we later looked at her will we found that one of her beneficiaries had been her niece Gertrude Rutherford, in whose home in Hunter's Road, Wimbledon, she had died.

From here we turned to read *The Vote*, the newspaper of the Women's Freedom League. Unexpectedly, once more the obituaries of *both* Baillie-Weavers turned up. Gertrude noted her long illness but also her long-standing involvement with the WFL, being a 'very early member' of it (*The Vote*, 10 December 1926, p. 360). Here, too, her gentle personality and courage are described but there is also information about her 'clear and logical mind', which made her 'a forcible convincing speaker', and her willing help at demonstrations and in meetings. No sleeping member of the WFL, then, but an involved and forcible one participating in various kinds of League political activities.

Harold Baillie-Weaver turned out to interest us a good deal more than we had expected. In Gertrude's obituary in *The Vote* he is referred to as 'our staunch friend . . . an active member of the Men's League for Women's Suffrage' (10 December 1926, p. 390).

His own obituary, which appeared some months earlier (*The Vote*, 2 April 1926, p. 106), notes that they lived at 'Eastward Ho! Wimbledon' and his failure to recover from his serious illness of 1925, and gives more information about his legal career: a law graduate of London University, he was called to the Bar at Lincoln's Inn in 1889. These is also an extremely appreciative outline of his own contribution to the suffrage cause. His strong personality is said to have been allied to a great administrative ability, which he used with 'justice and unselfish devotion to the cause of the suffering and the oppressed, which made him a great force in the movements which were dear to him'; these are outlined as humanitarianism, justice to animals and to children (how very British to couple them in this fashion), equal rights for women, peace and theosophy. His 'invaluable' work for the Men's League is noted, as is his general willingness to help other suffrage societies by 'speaking and writing'.

At this stage we were intrigued by the statement that Gertrude herself was involved in both the non-militant and the militant suffrage causes as well as being a pacifist. Also, I was fascinated by the very familiar collection of causes to which both Baillie-Weavers owed active allegiance – feminism, children's rights, animal rights coupled with vegetarianism, pacifism and theosophy – for, with the sole exception of theosophy, this combination has been thought by many to be something invented by late twentieth-century radicalism. However, although the fact that both Gertrude and Harold were involved in suffrage activities meant that a direct association with Emily Wilding Davison was more likely, knowing this took us no nearer being able to demonstrate that such an association actually existed. Ann briefly followed up various of the organisational involvements mentioned in the obituaries before we moved on to explore in more depth the feminist press, contacting London University and both the Theosophical Society and the National Anti-Vivisection Society (founded by another feminist, Frances Power Cobbe, in the 1880s).

From London University we found that Harold gained his law degree by private study, graduating in 1889 when he was twenty-eight (from which we were able to deduce – great minds at work! – that he was probably born in 1861 and died when he was about sixty-five). The General Secretary and Librarian of the Theosophical Society did much searching on our behalves and found in the

Theosophical Year Book of 1938 entries for both Gertrude and Harold, as well as copies of three of Gertrude's books in the library (*The Guest* (1917), *The Thunderbolt* (1919), and *A Brother of the Shadow* (1926)). Information on Gertrude was confined to the statement that she came from a Quaker family, and details of various of her books. Harold had been the General Secretary of the Theosophical Society from 1916 to 1921, as an administrator systematising its office work, and had also been involved in the Starry Cross, its anti-vivisection group. The General Secretary of the National Anti-Vivisection Society could unearth very little about either of the Baillie-Weavers for us apart from a letter written by Gertrude Colmore in 1910 that appeared in the organisation's journal (*Zoophilist and Animals' Defender*, December 1910), reprinted from the *Evening Standard* (29 October 1910). This deals with the ethical issues at stake in relation to vivisection; Gertrude suggests that ethics should proceed from a concern with principles and with means, not ends. The letter gains significance in relation to the moral/ethical underpinnings of feminism, certainly for Emily Wilding Davison and her friends, and probably for many of the other rank and file members of the wspu.

The *Suffrage Annual & Women's Who's Who* contained nothing about Gertrude Colmore beyond leading us to conjecture whether she might have been involved in the Women Writers' Suffrage League.[17] We thought this highly likely but we couldn't prove it. The directory of the *Englishwoman's Year Book* of 1913 contained an entry for her with an Essex address and nothing more.

It was the feminist newspapers of the period that provided us with most information about Gertrude Colmore. What we can add to the above is still disappointingly sparse, but certainly more than when our search began. We know from her obituary in *The Vote* that Gertrude was an early and continued to be an active member of the wfl. We have conjectured but been unable to establish firmly that she was a member of the wwsl. From our readings of *Votes For Women* and *The Suffragette* from 1907 to late 1918, we can now say with certainty that Gertrude was also an active wspu member both as Gertrude Colmore and as Gertrude Baillie-Weaver throughout this period.

In June 1909, two years after the founding of the wfl in which she was still active, Gertrude Baillie-Weaver spoke for the wspu at the Queen's Hall in Wimbledon, her co-speaker being Rose

Lamartine Yates (*VFW*, 25 June 1909, p. 847). Although we now know the point at which she and Harold Baillie-Weaver moved to Wimbledon, at this time we had simply gathered that it was not before 1912/1913: in October 1912 Gertrude contributed to the wspu fund, giving her wspu location as 'Cambridgeshire and District' (*The Suffragette*, 25 October 1912, p. 26), and in 1913 the *Englishwoman's Year Book* gave her address as 'of Essex'. The connection with the Wimbledon wspu branch and with Rose Lamartine Yates is significant in piecing together that patchwork of Emily's friendships and the genesis of the Colmore biography; and it is interesting that as early as 1909 Gertrude Colmore and Rose Lamartine Yates can be directly linked. In addition, a possible indirect link exists through their two husbands.

Both men were barristers, both were members of the Men's League, and both did work, of different kinds, for women's suffrage societies. Other members of the Men's League[18] included Henry Nevinson, the journalist and future husband of Evelyn Sharp; Lord Lytton, the brother of Con Lytton; the poet and future laureate John Masefield; the playwright Laurence Housman, and two men who were significant in Emily Wilding Davison's life and also her death: the Reverend Claud Hinscliff and Charles Mansell-Moullin.

Claud Hinscliff, as well as being an active member of the Men's League, was also the founder in 1909 and secretary of the Church League for Women's Suffrage. The Church League was an important suffrage organisation. First, the existence of a group of churchmen willing to speak and act on behalf of feminism (particularly – for this *was* Edwardian England – when they held high church office) lent moral force to the feminist cause.[19] Second, the Church League acted as an umbrella organisation for many women: militant members of the NUWSS, WFL and the wspu (for militancy, in the general sense of a willingness to make an open fuss, was at no point confined to the wspu) all met here and Emily Wilding Davison herself was a member, if not a particularly active one, of the Church League.

Hinscliff was one of the officiating clergy at Emily Davison's funeral service at St George's in Hart Street, Bloomsbury; another was the Reverend Baumgarten, whose church it was. Baumgarten too was an already active supporter of the militant cause – Sylvia Pankhurst (1931, p. 469) refers to him as 'a good friend of suffrage'. He made fairly regular contributions to the wspu fund through

1912 and 1913, and in 1914 he was still speaking in support of militancy (*The Suffragette*, 3 July 1914, p. 205).

The Men's League was basically a 'constitutional' suffrage organisation which eschewed militancy, though its members might and often did support that of others. However, in 1911 a militant men's suffrage group was founded after a series of preliminary meetings organised by Victor Duval, whose mother and sisters were all already active as WSPU militants. The Men's Union for Women's Enfranchisement, whose organising secretary Duval became, was formed in the wake of women being banned from most political meetings in case they turned out to be heckling suffragettes. As well as holding similar meetings to the Men's League, in which many Men's League members, such as Harold Baillie-Weaver, took part, members of the Men's Union took over the same role as the WSPU had done at political meetings, and received the same violent reactions previously meted out to women: broken bones and long periods of imprisonment for trivial and non-existent offences were not uncommon for Men's Union Members.

Charles Mansell-Moullin was the husband of another of Emily Wilding Davison's close friends, Edith Mansell-Moullin. He was a Harley Street doctor, a fellow of the Royal College of Surgeons and, for the period under discussion, its vice-president. He too was an active member of the Men's League (*MLWS Newssheet*, April 1912). As a doctor he spent much time and energy protesting in all possible ways against the barbarities and dangers of forcible feeding. His first public pronouncement about the dangers and iniquities of forcible feeding was made in 1909 (*VFW*, 1 October 1909, p. 2). In July 1912 he was the doctor who gave a detailed report of Emily Davison's injuries following her attempts to kill herself in Holloway prison on 21 June, and of the various injuries that had resulted from ten days' subsequent forcible feeding (*VFW*, 5 July 1912, p. 649).

The same issue of *Votes For Women* that gives details of his report contains information about a joint letter of protest against forcible feeding sent by a group of junior doctors to the Home Secretary, and also the reprint of a letter on the same topic that had appeared in the *British Medical Journal* of June 1912. In August Mansell-Moullin and two other doctors published a reasoned protest in *The Lancet* (Savill, Moullin & Horsley, 1912). As the senior medic involved in making such statements against government policy and practice in the treatment of feminist (and other) prisoners, he had considerably more to lose than most by doing so. In taking a public stand he laid his professional head on a line drawn by the Asquith government and by Home Secretary Reginald McKenna in particular. Speaking in the House of Commons, McKenna was swift to refute Mansell-Moullin's report in favour of that carried out in prison by a government appointee Crisp English (how very fitting a name!), and in doing so sneered at Mansell-Moullin's professional competence (*VFW*, 12 July 1912, p. 664).

Undeterred, Mansell-Moullin continued his public campaign against the government torture of militant women, incompletely disguised as feeding to save their lives, by pointing out various ways in which 'artificial' and 'forcible' feeding differed (*The Suffragette*, 4 April 1913, p. 405). Soon afterwards, acting with Frank Moxon, another doctor closely associated with the militant women (Kenney, 1924, pp. 218–19), he pointed out more evidence that the government campaign was actually one of systematic torture, this time focusing on the question of drugging militant prisoners (*The Suffragette*, 8 May 1914, p. 81; 12 June 1914, p. 141). And even before this he had known that the forcible feeding of Emily Davison during the long six-month sentence in Holloway that culminated in her 'suicide' attempt had occurred in the absence of any hunger strike by her – surely the clincher in any argument that forcible feeding was a mercy measure adopted only to stop suffragette women starving to death (indeed, Emily Davison was not the only woman subjected to this treatment).

Following Emily Davison's actions and injuries at the 1913 Derby she was taken to the cottage hospital at Epsom, near the race-course. The house surgeon nominally in charge of her was a Dr Peacock; but effectively it was Charles Mansell-Moullin who spent three days trying to save her life. She was brought to the hospital on Wednesday 4 June; on Friday 6 June he operated on her to provide some relief from the injuries to her head. This seemed to work, but she never regained consciousness and finally died on the afternoon of Sunday 8 June. His report on her injuries (*The Suffragette*, 13 June 1913, p. 578) was as follows:

> Miss Davison, who was completely unconscious, was taken at once to the Epsom Cottage Hospital. The shock of the injuries she had sustained was so severe that for some time it was not

thought that she would rally at all. On Thursday afternoon her pulse was a little better, but it was evident that there was bleeding going on inside the skull from a fracture across the base, and from the injured brain. On Friday an operation was performed which gave great temporary relief, but the injured portion of the brain never recovered, and the heart and the breathing gradually failed. Miss Davison was completely unconscious, never opening her eyes or speaking from the moment the horse struck her until the end. Dr Thornley and Dr Peacock showed her every possible attention, and the matron and staff were kindness itself.

Charles Mansell-Moullin and Harold Baillie-Weaver were two of the most active members of the Men's League. Harold's speaking engagements for the League brought him into close contact with various well-known WSPU women, including 'the leadership'. In April 1912 a speech he gave on 'Women and Evolution' at the London Pavilion had a full page coverage in *Votes For Women* (12 April 1912, p. 439). In December 1912, just after the 'Peth and Pank' split, he spoke at the London Pavilion again, this time with Mrs Pankhurst and Annie Kenney (*The Suffragette*, 16 December 1912, p. 134). Then in March 1913 he appeared with Evelyn Sharp (a key member of the banished Pethick-Lawrence group) at a WSPU 'At Home' in St John's Wood in London. It seems that the 'banishment' was at a national headquarters', and not at a local, WSPU level.

In April 1913, and in spite of his association with Evelyn Sharp, four consecutive issues of *The Suffragette* featured whole-page articles by him. The first dealt with the police raid on WSPU headquarters in April 1913 and particularly (how topical this sounds, given a similar police raid on the BBC during 1987) the fact that it was a 'fishing expedition' for which no proper warrant did or could exist (*The Suffragette*, 8 August 1913, p. 741). The second discussed the attempt at the Bow Street hearing later in April to declare WSPU objectives unlawful (*The Suffragette*, 15 April 1913, p. 757), and hence publishing its newspaper, distributing it, and donating money to it. If successful, this would have either completely suppressed the WSPU or driven it underground. The third pointed out that none of the four arrested and tried office staff had in any way determined either WSPU or *Suffragette* policy – that remained firmly in the hands of Christabel Pankhurst and was put into practice by Grace Roe (*The Suffragette*, 22 August 1913, p. 783).

The fourth and last article by Harold Baillie-Weaver referred to the operation of the 'Cat and Mouse' Act in the case of Mary Richardson,[20] pointing out that Dr Pearson, one of the medics involved in forcibly feeding her, 'threatened that . . . she would be kept until she was a physical and nervous wreck and then sent to an asylum' and noting 'the power of contemptuous arrogant men' convinced they are right in doing what they want against supposedly 'hysterical' women (*The Suffragette*, 29 August 1913, p. 803) – Harold, we concluded, was all right. This attempt to treat suffragettes as, or turn them into, madwomen was not confined to Mary Richardson: it had happened to Emily Wilding Davison in 1912, and to her close friend Mary Leigh.

Harold Baillie-Weaver's barrister colleague in the Men's Union, Thomas Lamartine Yates, similarly did not confine his activities to internal Men's Union matters. In October 1909 he was already acting as a legal adviser to WSPU women (see Rona Robertson to Thomas Lamartine Yates, 16 October 1909, Emily Wilding Davison papers, Fawcett Library), a role he continued until the war. He was arrested at least once, following the November 1911 mass window-smashing in London (*VFW*, 1 December 1911, p. 144). Also, sadly enough, it was he who represented Emily's mother at the inquest following her daughter's death. And the links roll on down the generations, for it was Ruth Yates, the widow of the Lamartine Yates' son Paul (born in 1908), who donated to the Fawcett Library the various possessions of Emily Wilding Davison that her mother-in-law, Emily's friend Rose, had kept after the inquest.

These involvements of Harold Baillie-Weaver, Charles Mansell-Moullin and the others are interesting in their own right, for they show something of the activities of some members of the under-researched men's suffrage organisations. We still did not know whether either of the Baillie-Weavers knew or had ever met Emily Wilding Davison. However, we had now discovered some more interesting material concerning Gertrude Colmore herself – or rather, Gertrude Colmore the writer.

Evelyn Sharp was a well-known writer of children's stories, a collector (and teller) of fairy stories and an active vice-president of the WWSL. While she was the paid WSPU Kensington organiser working from the shop at 143 Church Street in Kensington, she regularly ran bookstalls at WSPU fairs, exhibitions and bazaars. These bookstalls sold books donated by WWSL members (and often signed by them). Mrs Baillie-Weaver donated books (*VFW*, 22 December 1911, p. 196), which means that she was indeed likely to have been a WWSL member. More significantly, however, we found a large number of pieces of overtly militant suffragist fiction writing by Gertrude, whose obituary writer had said that her political allegiances could not be detected in any of her writing.

Votes For Women contained various fictional sketches by her, including 'Mr Jones and the governess' (16 August 1912, p. 743); 'George Lloyd' (16 May 1913, p. 471); 'Oh Richard' (4 July 1913, p. 589); 'Betsy' (10 October 1913, p. 557); 'Just This Once' (17 October 1913, p. 29); 'The Enormities of Eleanor' (14 November 1913, p. 91); 'The White Cross' (5 December 1913, p. 143); and 'Fellowship' (26 February 1915, p. 161). *The Suffragette* material includes the following sketches: 'The Introduction' (22 November 1912, p. 88, with a Woman's Press advertisement on the same page for books including *Suffragette Sally*); 'A Fool from Afar' (27 December 1912, p. 161); 'Pluck' (24 January 1913, p. 217; on the same page there is a note of a contribution to WSPU funds by, among others, G. Baillie-Weaver); 'The Shutter' (21 March 1913, p. 365); and the poem, 'Shame!' (25 April 1913, p. 473).

It's difficult not to think that the form of these sketches owes much to Olive Schreiner's use of the 'dreams' format in a number of works which were hugely popular among WSPU members.[21] In Colmore's sketches, too, characterisation and plot are almost completely absent; people are presented as the embodiment of very specific moral positions which come into conflict. Invariably, militant feminist meets uncomprehending but not necessarily evil manhood. The strength, conviction and sheer *goodness* of the feminist presence, makes the man see something of the error of his ways, even when he is very unwilling to admit this aloud.

The exception in some senses is 'Shame!', for although we meet the same abstracted, idealised militant feminist, here she is alone, in prison. She is the distilled essence of militant feminism, summing up all that is best and most noble in its beliefs and practices. The 'shameful' context is used as the basis of word-play, in which the emphasis is that she is 'A woman shameless and unashamed/One of a shameless band'.

These pieces of writing may not be great literature, but they *are* effective at the level of simple, heart-warming propaganda aimed at those already inside the militant movement. They are romances that tug at the heart if not at the mind (although we're in a small minority among our feminist contemporaries who would admit to being moved by such sentimental moral tales!). They are neatly written, make their points with economy and know not to labour the point. Gertrude was a craftswoman, good at her trade.

Gertrude and Harold joined the committee of *Votes For Women* in early 1915 (8 January 1915, p. 122). This was at a time when Gertrude was still active within the WFL and also in the rump of the WSPU that remained committed to a specifically feminist programme (this neglected aspect of WSPU history is discussed in the last chapter). Throughout the war and into 1919 both Baillie-Weavers continued to make regular financial contributions to the national funds of the WFL and to *Votes For Women*.

After the war Gertrude's animal rights work continued. With the Duchess of Hamilton she got Britain's first humane abattoir built, in Letchworth Garden City (the Theosophists already had connections in Letchworth). In the garden of St John's Lodge, Regent's Park, in London there is a commemoration of her and Harold's work in the form of a statue of a woman holding a lamb, which is inscribed 'To All Protectors of the Defenceless'.

We read *The Vote* later than the other feminist newspapers, when the above information had been assembled, and discovered that it was Gertrude Colmore who provided part of its coverage of Emily Davison's death and funeral (*The Vote*, 13 June 1913, pp. 112–14). She also wrote a piece on it for *Votes For Women* (20 June 1913, p. 554), so by then Gertrude was already conversant with many of 'the facts' of Emily's story. Was she asked to write *The Life* because of this? If so, by whom? Or did she herself suggest it? And to whom? Still no answers, but, late on in the writing of this manuscript, I came upon the fact that in September 1912 Grace Roe was the WSPU paid organiser of Cambridge and District (*VFW*, 27 September 1912, p. 838). And this was the very area in which Gertrude was then still living. A coincidence?

In the immediate aftermath of Emily Davison's death, Gertrude Colmore wrote a brief but telling piece entitled 'Unbalanced' (*The Vote*, 13 June 1913, p. 113). In this account of Emily's action it is very clear that Gertrude sees the public and the press, not Emily, as 'unbalanced', as disturbed, sick. To read *The Life* and 'Unbalanced' together is quite fascinating, for they show very clearly how the militant feminist community reacted to Emily Davison's Derby action and death and the negative portrayals of it that appeared in the national press.

At this point we had exhausted what could be discovered about Gertrude Colmore from the material then in our possession. So we turned our attention to discovering just who were Emily Davison's closest friends and colleagues, what kind of women they were and what kind of political allegiances they held.

Joan of Arc and the Horsewoman

The Suffragette of 13 June 1913 (p. 581) contains details of the funeral arrangements for Emily Wilding Davison and of the order of procession for escorting the hearse from Victoria Station through the streets of central London. Immediately in front of the hearse walked Emily's closest personal friends, behind the two banners proclaiming 'Thoughts have gone forth whose powers can sleep no more! Victory! Victory!' and 'Greater love hath no man than this, that he lay down his life for his friends' (which latter appeared on Emily's family gravestone).

Some secondary sources dealing with the death and funeral say there were six of these friends. This is a mistake which seems to derive from the conflation of two pieces of information. The first is the presence immediately behind the hearse and clearly visible in some photographs of the procession (Mackenzie, 1975, p. 241; and Fulford, 1967, facing p. 192) of the six women workers at WSPU headquarters who had been convicted of conspiracy a few days before and were braving (or inciting) arrest in the funeral procession (*The Suffragette*, 20 June 1913, pp. 591, 594). The second is the statement in the local Newcastle and Morpeth newspapers that six of Emily's comrades attended her coffin on the train and then stood vigil around it as it stood in Newcastle station overnight.

I certainly made this mistake, and spent much time gazing at the photograph of these six women, trying to drag their knowledge of Emily out of their distant faces. But later constant perusal and re-perusal of contemporary documents showed that this was wrong, that these were not her personal friends, for they went before and not behind the hearse.

The process of working out who her close friends were began with three sources. One was Antonia Raeburn's intriguing statement in *The Militant Suffragettes* (1973, p. 219) that

> Emily's friends, the familiar figures that had once been so outstanding – the Joan of Arc, the Bandleader and the Horsewoman – now walked beside the coffin as one.

Scouring the reports of endless WSPU marches, processions, bazaars and deputations, finally we decided who these women were. We concluded that 'Joan of Arc' was Elsie Howey, who often appeared dressed as Joan, in full armour and on horseback; 'the Bandleader' referred to Mary Leigh, the drum-major of the WSPU fife and drum band (which turned out in full band uniform in WSPU colours); 'the Horsewoman' defeated us for some time, but finally we concluded this must be Vera Holme, who, in riding habit and WSPU sash, rode from a WSPU meeting in June 1909 at Caxton Hall in London to the Houses of Parliament, with a message for Prime Minister Asquith.

The second source was the Colmore biography itself, discreet though it infuriatingly is as to personal details. For all it appears to tell us about the woman herself, readers will now be aware that Gertrude Colmore's book provides glowing abstractions about Emily but surprisingly little concrete information about who she knew and cared about – just a few names and sparse information about the women concerned, and some tantalising statements about 'friends' and 'companions'.

'A friend with whose family she used to stay' as a small child describes her as a 'pickle' (Colmore, 1913, p. 8). Miss Hitchcock, who was Headmistress at Kensington High School while Emily was there between the ages of thirteen and nineteen (1885–91), provides much of the information about her personality and appearance (Colmore, 1913, pp. 9, 49). 'The friend who was her constant companion', unlike Emily, was bored by musical comedy; she went with Emily to visit 'an old schoolfellow who had gone to Holloway College'; and this visit led to Emily wanting to go there too, which she did in 1891 (Colmore, 1913, p. 12). And then there was also the 'friend much with her in her militant days' (or was she the same one?) (Colmore, 1913, p. 19).

She writes to the 'old schoolfellow' in January 1913, following her arrest for the firing of pillar boxes, hoping she will not be disowned by her for being '*too* militant' (Colmore, 1913, p. 53). A letter written on 12 August 1909 from Longhorsley to an unnamed woman, who she thinks might actually be in Switzerland, notes that she and Mary Leigh got the longest sentences in Liverpool for helping to disrupt a Lloyd George meeting (Colmore, 1913, p. 22). And the night before the Derby incident she stood with Mary Leigh before a statue of Joan of Arc and refused to say what she intended to do at the Derby, telling Mary she should look in the evening paper (Colmore, 1913, pp. 55–6). She was arrested with Con Lytton in Newcastle in October 1909 but was eventually released without being charged – to her great chagrin (Colmore 1913, pp. 24–6).

Another *name* to add to Mary Leigh's is that of Mrs Penn Gaskell. She went with Emily to court in January 1912 (in connection with firing pillar boxes) and, although the many other women present were barred from the court, Emily called her as a witness (Colmore, 1913, pp. 42–3). And Emily went to the Penn Gaskells' home to be nursed when she was released from Holloway after attempting to kill herself (Colmore, 1913, pp. 49–50).

Colmore also mentions Miss Clarke (pp. 54–5), with whom Emily spent the evening of 3 June, attending a Toynbee Hall lecture, going to an ABC for tea, and 'being more affectionate than was her wont'. Apart from seeing the name from time to time, and wondering if she might be a relative of Mrs Pankhurst's sister Mrs Clarke, we have drawn a blank with Miss Clarke.

Our third source was the less tantalising, more concrete information contained in the 'Appreciations' that appeared in *The Suffragette* of 13 June 1913 (p. 580). 'The leaders' speak, in the brief statements of Mrs Pankhurst and Annie Kenney. Con Lytton, who knew Emily but probably not well, offers a similarly brief general appreciation of Emily as 'the truest upholder of our Great Cause'. The well-known scientist and long-term supporter of feminism Hertha Ayrton provides a longer, glowing but still impersonal statement about Emily, whose 'life is over, but her name will live for ever'. These are followed by three much more personal and touching statements by Edith Mansell-Moullin, E. Penn Gaskell and Rose Lamartine Yates.

Edith Mansell-Moullin says that she 'had the honour of Emily Davison's friendship for nearly four years' but before that her name was known to her because of the infamous Strangeways 'hosepipe' incident of October 1909 when Emily barricaded herself in her cell, to have six inches of icy water hosed into it on the order of the visiting magistrate. She says how she often asked Emily not to take any more risks, telling her she had done her share. She relates what Emily had told her about the Holloway 'suicide' incident: 'she told me how she could not endure the cries and moans of her fellow-sufferers'; and notes that she continually suffered physical pain as a consequence of what had happened. E. Penn Gaskell (we later discovered her name to be Elinor) wrote that Emily was one of the most wonderful people she had ever known, and, 'Knowing Emily Davison as I did, I can clearly read the meaning of this supreme sacrifice'. What Rose Lamartine Yates says, however, is more immediately moving. She 'stood with Mary Leigh by the bedside of our comrade, and my old college friend', thought of Emily freely giving whatever was hers for the women's movement, and remembered their college days together.

So: these three women had known Emily Davison well, and Rose was the schoolfriend who had been to Holloway College; to them we could add Mary Leigh as a close comrade and friend. More tentatively, not knowing the source for Antonia Raeburn's statement about 'Joan of Arc' and 'the Horsewoman', we could also count Elsie Howey and Vera Holme, at least at this stage. We set about assembling the biographies of these six women, building up a mosaic of brief mentions and glimpsed presences. This chapter took many times longer to piece together than any of the others, such is the state of published knowledge about the vast majority of feminist women in this period.[22]

I begin with the relatively brief information we have gathered about Elsie Howey and Vera Holme. Elsie Howey was one of the speakers at the June 1908 Hyde Park demonstration organised by the WSPU and *Votes For Women* provides potted biographies of all the speakers there (*VFW*, 18 June 1908). Wrongly named here as Elsie *Neville* Howey (the *Suffrage Annual & Women's Who's Who* of 1913 establishes her as Rose Elsie Nellie, poor thing), we are informed that she was born in 1884 in a Yorkshire village where her father was rector; after his death she and her mother moved to a village in Hertfordshire. I later discovered that her mother Gertrude had also been a WSPU member (MofL 57.70/18). After two years at St Andrews University in Scotland Elsie went to

Germany, where she realised 'women's position' and as a consequence soon 'threw herself into the women's movement'. She seems to have been first arrested in July 1908, with, among others, Mary Leigh (*VFW*, 9 July 1908, p. 298).

On 23 April 1909 *Votes For Women* featured an article by Evelyn Sharp (pp. 574–5) about the WSPU events held in London to celebrate the release of Emmeline Pethick-Lawrence from prison, which describes Elsie Howey appearing at the head of a mass procession as Joan of Arc (see also Pethick-Lawrence, 1938, p. 226). A large photograph of her on horseback, in full armour and open helmet, pennant flying, accompanies the article, a picture which is used over and over when either Joan or Elsie are written about (from now on I see Joan of Arc only in terms of Elsie's rendition of her!). On 5 September 1909 Asquith and Herbert Gladstone (at that point still Chancellor and Home Secretary respectively) were accosted by Elsie Howey, Jessie Kenney and Vera Wentworth (*VFW*, 10 September 1909, p. 1157).

In January 1910 during the general election Con Lytton, disguised as the 'Punch suffragette' Jane Warton, went to Liverpool and was arrested for throwing stones with two other WSPU members (who had recognised her and insisted on accompanying her), Mrs Nugent from Liverpool and Elsie Howey. She describes Elsie as 'a valiant as well as most dear one of our members' (Lytton, 1914, p. 247) and recounts how, both suffering from colds, they kept each other warm in the police station under the same blanket, Elsie telling anecdotes about her former imprisonments (Lytton, 1914, pp. 247–8). Elsie Howey was given a six-week sentence, 'Jane Warton' two weeks and Mrs Nugent was discharged (Lytton, 1914, pp. 249–61). On 11 February 1910 *Votes For Women* reported that she had just been released from prison (p. 308), with the Joan of Arc picture given prominent placing.

Until around 1913 Elsie Howey pops up regularly in the 'forthcoming meetings' section of *Votes For Women*. In the *Suffrage Annual & Women's Who's Who* she describes herself as an unpaid organiser for the WSPU, and says that her hobbies are riding and hockey. Following Emily Davison's firing of pillar boxes (see the Militancy chapter for a detailed account of this), many other women carried out arson attacks (some of which I doubt Emily would have approved). In December 1912 many false alarm calls were made to the London Fire Brigade. Elsie Howey was arrested for one of these in Holland Park on Wednesday 11 December (*VFW*, 13 December 1912, p. 165). Faced with a 20*s* fine or two months imprisonment, she elected to go to prison. Our last sight of her before the war was the statement that she had been imprisoned and forcibly fed at some point in 1913 (*The Suffragette*, 2 January 1914, p. 274).

Elsie Howey comes across as brave, outgoing, sometimes over-enthusiastic and a bit unthinking, and perhaps rather hearty. On the slim evidence of Con Lytton's complimentary remarks about her, it may be that she matured into greater sensitivity in 1913 as her thirtieth birthday approached; otherwise any friendship between her and Emily Davison seems most unlikely. Emily had no interest in horses, although she clearly had great respect for bravery, given the feelings she had about Mary Leigh. She was interested in literature and the arts and in 'spirituality', none of which are mentioned in connection with Elsie Howey (but of course this could be the product of an insufficiency of information, rather than because Elsie was actually a 'hearty' and nothing else). However, it's worth noting that we have found no evidence for the existence of this as a close friendship beyond Antonia Raeburn's remark about 'Joan of Arc' at Emily's funeral.

A close friendship with Vera Holme seems equally or even more unlikely. Vera Holme appears on the WSPU scene in 1909 as a member of the Actresses' Franchise League who had appeared in minor Gilbert and Sullivan roles at the London Savoy (Raeburn, 1973, p. 101). On 29 June 1909 a Women's Parliament was held in Caxton Hall and sent many small deputations to the House of Commons to protest at the failure to fulfil the Bill of Rights and allow Mrs Pankhurst to petition the King. Before the first deputation set off, Vera Holme in riding dress and WSPU sash rode on horseback from Caxton Hall to St Stephen's Square with a message for the Prime Minister; she was stopped and turned away, and so cantered back (Raeburn, 1973, p. 109).

In *Votes For Women* of 17 June 1910 she is noted as one of the two mounted marshalls at the Hyde Park demonstration due to take place in July 1910 (p. 609). Soon after this she became chauffeur to Mrs Pankhurst. Originally she had been thought too young and 'giddy' for the job ('she wasn't at all for having me because I used to act the galoot in the office'), even though Emmeline Pethick-Lawrence had wanted her to have it; later she got much amusement from being assumed to be a man by maids at houses she drove to

(Raeburn, 1973, pp. 110–11).

I later discovered (MofL 73.83/59 (c) pp. 17–18) that Vera Holme was born in 1882 in Yorkshire and died in 1969. In 1914 she joined the Scottish Women's Hospitals organisation and went to Yugoslavia. After the war she lived in Scotland with Margaret Greenless and Margaret Ker. A close friend of Edy Craig, Ellen Terry's feminist daughter, she helped to organise the annual Ellen Terry memorial performance in Kent. When older she was a stalwart not only of her local drama club but also of the Women's Institute. Known universally as Jack, she was also an expert 'fly-fisherman'.

Militant suffragism, like time and death, was said to be a great leveller: duchesses reputedly marched in demonstrations side by side with parlour-maids. But it is still difficult to imagine a close friendship between Emily Davison and Vera Holme or between Emily and Elsie Howey. This is not intellectual snobbery; rather it is because there seems a political gulf between these two reputedly close friendships and Emily's four other close friendships, with Mary Leigh, Edith Mansell-Moullin, Elinor Penn Gaskell and Rose Lamartine Yates.

Mrs Leigh enters the arena

David Mitchell describes Emily Davison and Mary Leigh (and also Charlotte Marsh and Sylvia Pankhurst) as the 'freelance militants', guerrilla activists (Mitchell, 1977, p. 321). As Colmore had noted (1913, p. 52), Emily Davison had a habit of pioneering militant action without recourse to leadership approval or even knowledge, and this was 'incompatible with employment by the WSPU'. Sylvia Pankhurst writes that not only was Emily's firing of pillar boxes in 1912 'cold-shouldered by Clements Inn at the time' (Pankhurst, 1931, p. 362), but also that she was 'condemned and ostracised as a self-willed person who persisted in acting upon her own initiative without waiting for official instructions' (Pankhurst, 1931, p. 315). It's difficult not to think that here Sylvia is writing as much about herself as about Emily Davison; however, it was certainly true as a statement about Emily's relationship with 'the leadership'.

Emily was her own woman, 'unorthodox' and thus an unreliable follower because she acted on her own principles, for her own reasons, and as and when *she* thought appropriate. This was a characteristic she shared with Mary Leigh but with different consequences for their public, if not private, relationship with the wspu leadership.

In May 1908 Mary Leigh was already active as a wspu militant, as the potted biographies of speakers at the Hyde Park demonstration provided by *Votes For Women* of 18 June 1908 (pp. 251–4) describe. She did by-election work on behalf of the wspu and by May 1908 had already been imprisoned once in Holloway. She was imprisoned again in July 1908, with Edith New, for throwing stones at the windows of 10 Downing Street (*VFW*, 9 July 1908, p. 298), and was released in August 1908. This was the first stone-throwing incident and it was undertaken without the knowledge of the leadership. Mrs Pankhurst noted that having 'acted without orders', they would not have resented their action being disowned by headquarters (Pankhurst, 1914, p. 228), although in fact she entirely approved. The pioneering militant act was carried out as the most serious protest they could make against the very stiff sentences given to wspu women following the arrest of deputations attempting to get to the House of Commons (Pethick-Lawrence, 1938, pp. 185–6).

In January 1909 a meeting to honour Mrs Pankhurst and Mary Leigh was held in the Queen's Hall in London (*VFW*, 21 January 1909, pp. 276–7); Mary Leigh had been imprisoned three times during 1908 and had spent more than six months of the year in prison. She had a habit of ducking out of such valedictory meetings and did on this occasion. Her reasons for avoiding them, characteristically, were stated for her by others: it seems that Mary Leigh believed in democracy through and through; she had no liking for personality cults and, as she saw it, unwarranted admiration for simply carrying out her principles and doing her duty.

In May 1909 Mary Leigh was back in wspu news, this time for something less serious: she had become the drum major of the wspu drum and fife band, 'carrying the handsome silver mace in truly martial fashion' (*VFW*, 21 May 1909, p. 693); the band soon became much in demand for marches and processions.

The stone-throwing incident was not the only time Mary Leigh undertook freelance militant action or was the cause of new militant initiatives in official and wspu rank-and-file response. In September 1909 she and Charlotte Marsh threw slates from a nearby roof towards the hall where a meeting was being held by Prime Minister

Asquith in Birmingham. Following this she was the first among a group of WSPU prisoners to be forcibly fed – the first occasion that militant suffragettes were subjected to this treatment in Britain.

Charles Mansell-Moullin spoke out against this forcible feeding as a calculated brutality against 'Mrs Leigh, Miss Marsh and the other Suffragette prisoners' (*VFW*, 1 October 1909, p. 2). Two weeks later, a lengthy statement about Mary Leigh's experiences was published (*VFW*, 15 October 1909, p. 34). Con Lytton was arrested with Emily Davison in Newcastle that October following a personal protest at the forcible feeding of Mary Leigh (*VFW*, 15 October 1909, p. 36):

> When she realised that a working woman . . . had been sentenced . . . and was being tortured . . . she magnificently resolved, as the daughter and sister of a peer of the realm . . . challenges the Government to treat her as they have treated the body of her sister, a working woman.

By November 1909, when Mary Leigh started her court action against the authorities because of the forcible feeding, the leadership had opened a Mary Leigh Defence Fund (*VFW*, 12 November 1909, p. 105), and she joined the select band of WSPU women of whom official post-cards were sold (*VFW*, 26 November 1909, p. 130).

Thus this cycle of events was started in 1908 when Mary Leigh and Edith New made a protest about the treatment of some of their colleagues; as a consequence they were treated in an even more repressive way. This led to Con Lytton's militant action in 1909 and 1910 and in June 1912 Emily Davison's protest at the treatment of women in Holloway. Five days after this, mass window-smashing took place in London as 'A women's protest against the Government that tortures women!' (Raeburn, 1973, p. 176), and horrifying stories about what was happening to suffragette prisoners were circulating in (and outside) the militant press.

When Asquith was in Dublin on an official visit in July 1912 feminists demonstrated and violent scenes took place between them and the police. In the mêlée Mary Leigh symbolically placed a small hatchet in Asquith's carriage. Later that evening, having avoided arrest, she and Gladys Evans set fire to the curtains at the Theatre Royal as the audience was leaving. They were arrested, tried and given five-year sentences for the Theatre Royal charge only. Two other women, Jennie Baines and Mabel Capper (both of whom had long and active political careers as feminists, socialists and pacifists in Newcastle and Manchester respectively), received lesser sentences (these events can be followed in *VFW*, 9 August 1912, pp. 728–30; 16 August 1912, pp. 741–9; 23 August 1912, p. 765; 30 August 1912, p. 772; 6 September 1912, p. 784; 13 August 1912, p. 797).

When Mary Leigh and Gladys Evans were first in prison rumours circulated that attempts were to be made to certify Mary Leigh for lunacy.[23] Grace Roe (an Irishwoman) was sent to Dublin by the WSPU to look after the interests of Mary Leigh and Gladys Evans; she reported on an interview she had had with the Lord Lieutenant of Ireland (*VFW*, 6 September 1912, p. 784), who said that

. . . he thinks Mrs Leigh must be mad, and he has given me to understand she may be put in an asylum . . . it would be almost impossible to get her released from there.

A separate trial of the 'hatchet' incident took place in December 1912. The difference between Mary Leigh's courtroom account of her actions and the description of them in police evidence and from there in contemporary newspapers illustrates how the press – at the kindest – got things wrong or – at the unkindest – systematically misreported feminist activity. Mary Leigh was refused leave to call an important witness, John Redmond, a cabinet minister and leader of the Irish Party, whom she was accused of having injured by her action. Speaking in her defence, she noted that she had been described as having thrown a hatchet into Asquith's carriage and so seriously hurting John Redmond's head (*The Suffragette*, 20 December 1912, p. 152).

. . . she admitted that she was the woman who 'put' the implement into the carriage. She did not throw it. She simply 'put' it into the carriage. Therefore it was impossible that Mr Redmond's injuries were received by her hand . . . The hatchet was used in a symbolic manner . . . even in the past . . . such things as hatchets were used. It was used, she continued, as a symbol to show that people, if they became despotic, and steeped themselves in certain procedure, can be likened to an absolute oligarchy. It was her intention . . . to show those people the significance of her action . . . If she had had any intention of doing an injury she should have made no mistake in the matter.

The jury failed to agree, presumably not convinced by the interpretation put on John Redmond's statement by the police but impressed with Mary Leigh's superbly argued defence statement (unlike the judge, who castigated her for it). Mary Leigh was re-tried and this time she was convicted.

As this interlinked series of incidents shows, 'freelance' militancy was in its origins (before it was coordinated, orchestrated and formalised by the wspu leadership in spring 1913) the product at least as much of personal/political relationships between particular feminist women as of abstracted principle. Indeed the principles of such women were not abstracted, but firmly rooted in their highly political everyday lives and in what was happening to their militant comrades. As Emmeline Pethick-Lawrence notes in relation to the Asquith 'hatchet' incident (1938, p. 187):

> On this and other occasions many new developments of militancy were initiated by generous-minded and courageous individuals, who won admiration and imitation from others.

Edith New had earlier spoken of her own peaceful disposition which, she wryly but fondly noted, was 'Unlike her brave comrade, Mrs Leigh' (*VFW*, 27 August 1908, p. 406). An account of Mary Leigh being sentenced in late December 1911 describes her as a small woman, slight and pale, who really couldn't have done what she was accused of (*VFW*, 29 December 1911, p. 212). I personally believe that she could have done anything she set her mind to, as a brief account of three incidents may convey.

The local Basingstoke newspaper (reprinted in *VFW*, 30 June 1911, p. 651) reported that Mary Leigh was the main speaker at a public meeting in the Market Square. A boy threw a stone which hit her on the head:

> Without an instant's hesitation, Mrs Leigh leapt from the waggonette, caught the boy by the collar, held him till he humbly apologised before the crowd, released him, and was back in the wagonette before the astonished audience realised what a narrow escape she had had.

I tend to think it was the boy that had had the narrow escape. A long account of Mrs Leigh during the Dublin events (*VFW*, 16 August 1912, p. 749) similarly notes her courage and agility: being pursued by a group of hostile men, she jumped out of the conveyance she was in, charged and routed them. Mary Leigh was by no means the only one of Emily Davison's friends who ignored 'leadership' injunctions to stop working with Sylvia Pankhurst in the East End of London. At a public meeting in October 1913 Sylvia – 'on license' and there in disguise – at one point stood up and revealed herself to the crowd and the assembled police. When the police moved in to arrest her,

> Mrs Leigh advanced to the front of the platform and waving her arms exhorted 'Rise up People'. The audience rushed forward, many of them carrying chairs, which they threw at the police. Mrs Leigh was seized and dragged from the platform . . . had been badly handled . . . was subsequently released (*The Times*, 14 October 1913, p. 4).

During Mrs Leigh's imprisonment in Mountjoy prison in 1912, Lawrence Houseman dedicated a verse to her which contained the lines 'She won because she had the will/To die – she whom they dared not kill! . . . One poor weak body beat them all!' (Raeburn, 1973, p. 179). As verse this is not impressive; as a tribute to Mary Leigh's courage it is. And Emmeline Pethick-Lawrence (1938, p. 244) later added to this characterisation:

> Mary Leigh was notable amongst us all for her great courage. Her calm and quiet demeanour seemed to add to her moral strength.

A brave woman, then; one with so great a reputation among other WSPU women that the less-than-admiring leadership had to turn a blind eye to her unpredictability. The aftermath of Dublin left *Votes For Women* wallowing in page after page of praises for Mrs Leigh. In a fascinating and mischievous, but very telling, article in *The Freewoman* (22 August 1913, pp. 263–4) Dora Marsden (formerly a WSPU paid organiser herself) says that

> the impertinences meant to be eulogies . . . are nicely calculated to bring on a bad attack of nausea . . . So swiftly does a daring deed and fully-shouldered responsibility turn an aforenamed traitor into a heroine!

She points out that Mary Leigh knew she was disliked by the leadership but refused to leave the WSPU because she saw it as '*her* Union, which she has helped to build up into power by the passion of her soul and the untellable hardships she has undergone'.

There is later evidence of the same independence of mind and action, the same refusal to accept authority where she deemed it illegitimate, the same bravery in facing situations that others wouldn't. In an interview with David Mitchell in 1965, Mary Leigh describes going several times to France in the months after Emily's death to tick off Christabel Pankhurst. On one of these occasions (Mitchell, 1977, p. 218)

> I said the militants were loyal but sick of taking orders from young office girls while the leaders were in prison and Christabel in Paris.

Mary Leigh obviously shared Dora Marsden's feelings about 'leaders' who led so resolutely from behind, and didn't mind saying so. To no avail of course, but that didn't stop her from trying again later.

Mary Leigh, then, was a woman who was calm and quiet in the face of repression, but who struck back with all her powers. A woman with moral strength, who acted on the basis of principle and didn't stop to count the cost. A woman who recognised no 'leaders' with any prerogative to demand obedience from her where this cut against her principles and her perceptions of what was going on. It seems to me that Mary Leigh embodied the qualities which Emily Wilding Davison most admired and attempted to put into practice in her own life.

And Mary Leigh did not forget Emily. She visited her bedside with Rose Lamartine Yates as Emily was dying, as I've already noted. She was also the founder of the Emily Davison Lodge (MofL 26069/3) and arranged for flowers to be placed on Emily's grave through a local Morpeth florist for many years until her own death. In a record of a memorial meeting of the Emily Davison Lodge on 9 June 1921, a resolution was passed detesting the terrorism used by the British government to exterminate the Irish people and also demanding the withdrawal of British armed forces from Ireland, Egypt and India (Emily Wilding Davison papers, Fawcett Library). Emily, as I later explain, would have approved.

A later visit to the Suffragette Collection in the Museum of London revealed further information about Mary Leigh (MofL 57.116/22; 73.83/49). She was born in 1885 in Manchester and was a teacher before her marriage to Mr Leigh, a builder. During the First World War, Mary Leigh became an ambulance driver in this country, but had to revert to her pre-marriage name because of her record as a 'trouble-maker'. After the war she lived for many years in Sunbury-on-Thames before moving back to London. When she went every year to Emily's grave she took with her the flag Emily had had with her at the Derby. Mary had also marched with it on the first Aldermarston march. A fervent socialist, she attended every May Day parade in Hyde Park, in WSPU regalia and carrying Emily's flag. And her 'trouble-making' continued, I'm glad to say.

In 1924 she was imprisoned for the last time for punching a policeman who had knocked her into the gutter – she had been writing on the pavement information about Emily Davison's memorial meeting that year. When David Mitchell interviewed her in 1965 she had recently been thrown out of the House of Commons for heckling during a debate on pensions. Interestingly, Mitchell's notes end with the information that in 1908 in Holloway Mary Leigh remembered Christabel Pankhurst whispering, 'I'm not coming to prison again. It's a waste of time.' And of course she didn't.

Reconstructing Edith, Elinor and Rose

Edith Mansell-Moullin remained a mystery for a considerable time. She was initially involved in the settlement movement, and later she and Charlotte Despard were active at the WFL Nine Elms settlement. At the same time that her husband Charles began to speak out against forcible feeding and became involved in the Men's League she began to contribute to the WSPU fund (*VFW*, 12 November 1909, p. 105). There are relatively few mentions of her apart from her donations, but she must have been very much more involved than this suggests. *Votes For Women* of 28 January 1910 reports that Mrs Mansell was violently ejected from a campaign meeting in Dundee for the Liberal election candidate Winston Churchill (p. 283) (this could have been the confusingly similarly named Mrs Mildred Mansel). Then *Votes For Women* (22 July 1910, p. 711) notes that Edith Mansell-Moullin spoke on Platform 1 at the 1910 Hyde Park demonstration. Platform 1 was chaired by Mrs Pankhurst. Speakers on it were Mrs Pankhurst herself, Mabel Tuke, one of her close colleagues in the WSPU, and Edith Mansell-Moullin. Select company, then.

The potted biography of Edith Mansell-Moullin contains little more than the statement that she 'Worked among poor and among sweated women since her girlhood'. Later I found (MofL 57.116/79) that as a very young woman she had been involved on the periphery of the docks strike and also of the match girls strike organised by Annie Besant; that she was an active member of the Anti-Sweating League, and a frequent visitor to the Kensington wspu. This draws in a connection with Louisa Eates, who spoke on Platform 36 at the same Hyde Park demonstration. The biography of Louisa Eates says that one of her major concerns was the situation of women workers as well as being honorary (i.e. unpaid) secretary in the 'active Kensington Union' (*VFW*, 22 July 1910, p. 714). Another account notes Edith Mansell-Moullin's involvement with the Women's Industrial Council (*VFW*, 9 April 1909, p. 534), while I later found that at one point she had been the secretary of its very influential Investigating Committee (MofL 58.87/65).

Relatively low-key but none the less 'militant' involvement in wspu activities characterises Edith Mansell-Moullin's career within it. On 21 November 1911 she was on the platform at a Caxton Hall meeting which passed resolutions to be taken to the House of Commons (MacKenzie, 1975, p. 179). Two days later, she can be glimpsed waiting to be tried at Bow Street police station with Con Lytton, Mrs Haverfield and some 217 other women arrested after that meeting, and then in prison afterwards (Lytton, 1914, pp. 326–33).

In January 1913 Edith was still giving money to wspu funds (*The Suffragette*, 24 January 1913, p. 217). In June 1913 in the aftermath of Emily's death and funeral (and, indeed, before it) there were serious fears that Mrs Pankhurst might die as the result of the operations of the Cat and Mouse Act. Much protest about the Act was made, even by eminently 'respectable' men, but McKenna was seemingly impervious; Antonia Raeburn quotes some verses Edith produced in July 1913 as a description of one such encounter between McKenna and a male critic of the Act (Raeburn, 1973, pp. 205–6). Later that month at a London Pavilion meeting chaired by Edith Mansell-Moullin, Mrs Pankhurst, out on licence from prison and hunger and thirst strike, made a surprise appearance after Annie Kenney had finished speaking (*The Suffragette*, 18 July 1913, pp. 678–9). Our last sight of Edith at this stage of the research was organising a meeting of the Forward Cymric (Welsh) Suffrage

Union[24] in June 1914 in protest at the continual cat-and-mousing of Sylvia Pankhurst (Pankhurst, 1931, pp. 438–54). Later I found (MofL 57.116/79) that she had left the WSPU in 1913 (for unspecified reasons), had been an active pacifist, and for many years had been a worker for the blind at St Dunstan's as well as for the GCR (we have not yet discovered what these initials stand for).

In her appreciation of Emily Davison, Edith Mansell-Moullin wrote that she knew Emily for four years and that she thought it was a privilege to have had the friendship of a woman who was so brave, daring and courageous. Emily had discussed the Holloway incident with her in terms of sacrifice to put an end to horror; Edith had said that Emily had done her share of dangerous activities, but Emily had responded that 'enough' would come only after 'the vote' had been achieved (*The Suffragette*, 13 June 1913, p. 580).

The tone of the appreciation suggests something of what the basis of her relationship with Emily might have been. There seems to be a rather one-sided admiration (but it's necessary of course to keep firmly in mind that Emily's is the one voice that cannot speak, 'in appreciation' or otherwise, of her friends). There is also a shared concern with 'spirituality', with the moral basis of feminist – and other – action.

In the concluding paragraph of her appreciation, Edith refers to Emily Davison as a martyr, notes that martyrs voluntarily lay down their lives for a cause, and hopes that there may be 'much searching of heart among the leaders of Church and State and Society' that a woman such as Emily gave her life to rouse them from 'their blindness and their apathy'. Conventional WSPU rhetoric on one level, but something about its reference to martyrs, holy causes, sacrifices and an apathetic church suggests that, like Emily Davison in some of her writing, Edith Mansell-Moullin thought within a frame of reference, language and symbolism supplied by Christianity but departed radically from its orthodox and state-promulgated forms, rejecting 'the Church' as part of the conventional and anti-female social order.

To tie some of these 'loose ends' about ethics, spirituality and politics together requires an account of the remaining two of Emily Davison's close friends, Elinor Penn Gaskell and Rose Lamartine Yates, and then a discussion of militancy as displayed in Emily Davison's writings and public actions. As the lives of these two women touch on each other, and on Emily's, in a more apparent way than those of the four women discussed above, their activities are described in tandem. In piecing this patchwork together we found that following Rose into the deepest recesses of Wimbledon reveals not only the fate of the Women's Record House, but also something more of the histories of Harold Baillie-Weaver and Gertrude Colmore.

The first mention of a WSPU branch in Wimbledon appears in *Votes For Women* of 28 November 1908 (p. 158). In February 1909 Rose Lamartine Yates' name is recorded for the first time; she was arrested and appeared at Bow Street, first alone and then in company with Con Lytton and twenty-seven other women arrested following a deputation (*VFW*, 26 February 1909, p. 382; 2 April 1909, p. 499). A further report (5 March 1909, p. 407) provides information of her speech in court, in which she insisted that the law of liberty was higher than that made by men and governments. She mentioned her son Paul, aged eight months – a very human touch in that setting – and said that both she and her husband agreed that she would blush before the child if she hadn't gone on the deputation. Her decision to do so was also influenced by her great admiration for Emmeline Pethick-Lawrence. According to the article, her husband was a solicitor, she was educated 'abroad' and at Holloway College, was proficient in modern languages and was a council member of the national cycling organisation.

The aftermath of her first prison experience was a busy time for Rose Lamartine Yates. In early April 1909 she spoke at the dinner given in honour of the released prisoners at the Inns of Court Hotel. As a 'busy woman with many public duties and little leisure', she had expected that prison, and solitary confinement in particular, would have given her the opportunity for reflection and thought, but instead it had had a 'numbing' effect on her mind (*VFW*, 2 April 1909, p. 499).

Later that month Rose Lamartine Yates and Mary Gawthorpe spoke in Manchester on 'prison life'. This was the first of a number of occasions on which they worked together, and they later became close friends (*VFW*, 30 April 1909, p. 603; 7 May 1909, p. 631; Gawthorpe, 1952, pp. 37–8). In May, Rose made the first appearance that we could find at a Wimbledon WSPU meeting (*VFW*, 7 May 1909, p. 631). An earlier letter from her appeared in *Votes For Women* of 23 April 1909 (p. 569) offering to put up placards advertising the newspaper on the walls of her courtyards and outbuildings and to plant WSPU flags on her hayricks, all of which could be easily seen by travellers on the London to Portsmouth Road. The address given is 'Dorset Hall, Merton'.[25] Our Rose, son Paul and obliging solicitor husband did not live in straightened circumstances.

In mid-May 1909 Rose made a collection at an exhibition organised by the Wimbledon WSPU which was attended by hundreds of people from all over London – at which Mary Leigh and the WSPU drum and fife band appeared (*VFW*, 21 May 1909, p. 708). June and July brought something momentous for our investigation of the web of friendship around Emily Davison. At the Queen's Hall in Wimbledon in late June Rose and Mrs Baillie-Weaver spoke at a WSPU meeting (*VFW*, 25 June 1909, p. 847), while during July speakers at a Wimbledon WSPU meeting were Rose and Harold Baillie-Weaver (*VFW*, 5 July 1909, p. 892). So Rose knew both Harold and Gertrude, and as early as mid-1909.

In January 1910 Rose chaired her first Wimbledon WSPU meeting (*VFW*, 7 January 1910, p. 236), while during February, March and April of that year she gave a series of addresses to the Wimbledon Union which were reported (by her) in the pages of the *Wimbledon Borough News*. Indeed, she wrote a regular WSPU column in the *News* from February 1910 until the First World War brought the cessation of militant feminist activity.

In April 1910 we found the first concrete evidence of a connection between Rose Lamartine Yates and Elinor Penn Gaskell: they spoke together at a London meeting at which Emmeline-Pethick-Lawrence also spoke (*VFW*, 15 April 1910, p. 464). At this point, not long before the mass WSPU Hyde Park demonstration of 1910, Elinor Penn Gaskell needs to be brought more definitely into the story.

The first 'spotting' of Elinor Penn Gaskell comes in June 1908, when she gave money to the WSPU fund (*VFW*, 18 June 1908, p. 253); the following year similar sums, usually of a few shillings or a pound or two, were donated by her at intervals. Unlike Rose, there is no sudden surge of public militant action, but a quiet involvement that gradually led her (during the second half of 1908 until 1915) into speaking on behalf of the WSPU at various locations in London. The decision to remain 'unmilitant' may not have been made willingly by her. In June 1909 *Votes For Women* printed a letter in which 'Mr and Mrs Penn Gaskell' donated £40 to funds in lieu of

Elinor not going on a deputation, then 'we' became more obviously the voice of Mr Penn Gaskell: 'I should like it to be known how earnestly she wished to join this deputation. Had she alone been concerned, no obstacles would have sufficed to deter her' (*VFW*, 25 June 1909, p. 856).

This was the same deputation that led to Rose Lamartine Yates' arrest; it is tempting to think that Elinor and Rose knew each other at this stage and that the meeting they both spoke at in April 1910 might have been the result of an existing friendship. Be that as it may, it is certain that Elinor Penn Gaskell did not condemn what she understood as militancy. *Votes For Women* of 21 January 1910 (p. 262) carries an open letter from her 'To one who condemns violence', in which she points out that violence is in fact the *response* to so-called militancy, and argues that militancy is morally and practically entirely justified. Perhaps by this stage her husband had learnt better than to stop Elinor doing things she felt strongly about!

From early 1909 through to 1914 mentions of Elinor Penn Gaskell come thick and fast. Some weeks she addressed as many as five public meetings all over London, and she rarely did less than one or two public meetings a week. She was a speaker at the Hyde Park demonstration in 1910 and in fact chaired Platform 14. She must have been a valued worker indeed. Her biography states (*VFW*, 22 July 1910, p. 712) that she had been connected with 'social work and social reform' for a long time.[26] Elinor was the honorary (i.e. unpaid) secretary of the North-West London (later Kilburn) wspu in which she was an active worker. She was also 'keenly interested in all societies which aim at the protection of animals'. At this point both of our minds leapt to the Baillie-Weavers, of course (and we later found that this concern for animal rights was also shared by Emily Davison). A small portrait of Elinor, as of a number of the other speakers including Mary Leigh, appears with the article: she looks straight into the camera, imposingly massive in appearance.

Emily Davison and Rose Lamartine Yates spoke at the Hyde Park demonstration as well. Rose is described (*VFW*, 22 July 1910, p. 714) as having been imprisoned with Mrs Pethick-Lawrence; it also states that she had 'studied much', particularly modern languages, was 'a keen gardener, poultry rearer, and housewife, and takes a prominent part in public work'. Interestingly, like Emily Davison, Rose Lamartine Yates describes herself in a combination of academic and activist terms. In Rose's case, we find the 'highest examination' but also 'served imprisonment'; in Emily's, 'higher examinations' and 'Oxford Final Honours School' but also 'numerous imprisonments' and 'protest against forcible feeding'. At a guess, Rose and Emily shared a very similar world-view, albeit from rather different social vantage points: Rose was monied and married, Emily had no visible source of income and no visible partnership relationships of any kind.

Votes For Women of 2 September 1910 (p. 792) contains a fairly lengthy report from Elinor Penn Gaskell as secretary of the North-West London WSPU branch, which gives her address as 12 Nicholl Road, Willesden. Her association with the Kilburn/North-West London WSPU continued until the First World War – indeed until the meetings in late 1917 protesting at the pro-war hijacking of the WSPU by the Pankhurst leadership.

At various points from 1910, Elinor spoke at Wimbledon and Rose at Kilburn. However, the Wimbledon WSPU remains more significant, for at least twice in May 1910 Emily Davison came to speak at public meetings chaired by Rose (*VFW*, 13 May 1910, p. 554; 27 May 1910, p. 568); and the association continued, for *The Suffragette* of 1 November 1912 (p. 42) reports that Emily spoke at public meetings in Wimbledon every Sunday.

The centre of WSPU war-time opposition to the Pankhurst leadership was a group which included all Emily Davison's close friends. A number of meetings were organised during 1915 by WSPU and ex-WSPU members to protest about the way in which the Pankhurst leadership had fundamentally changed WSPU policy: the organisation no longer had feminist or even suffragist aims, had overturned its anti-war stance, and had changed *The Suffragette/The Britannia* in line with new policy. A further criticism was the failure to account for any of the large sum of WSPU money that remained unspent in leadership hands.[27]

One such meeting was held on 22 October 1915 in Caxton Hall in London, scene of so many WSPU meetings (Rosen, 1974, p. 253 quoting the *Daily News*, 18 November 1915). It was chaired by Rose Lamartine Yates and a resolution was passed protesting that the WSPU name was no longer used to 'remedy the innumerable disabilities on unenfranchised womanhood', and calling for properly audited accounts. Copies of this resolution were sent to Christabel and Mrs Pankhurst. A similar meeting was held soon after in Brondesbury Hall in Kilburn, chaired by Elinor Penn Gaskell. It adopted a manifesto reaffirming feminist and pacifist principles and covering similar ground to the Caxton Hall resolution: the leadership's misuse of the WSPU name and failure to account for funds (Rosen, 1974, p. 253).

This time there was a response: Mrs Pankhurst's reasons as to why there could be no report or balance sheet were reported in the *Weekly Dispatch* of 3 December 1915 (quoted in Rosen 1974, p. 253). In fact, neither question was settled until mid-1917, when money from the funds was used to set up an adoption home for girls and the Pankhurst part of the WSPU changed its name to The Women's Party.

By the time all this information about Elinor Penn Gaskell and Rose Lamartine Yates had been pieced together, Ann had become particularly interested in Rose, mainly because she lived in Wimbledon and was the source of the connection with Harold Baillie-Weaver and Gertrude Colmore. If possible, we wanted to find out more about this connection. Wimbledon and its long-established local newspaper was Ann's immediate reference point.

From 1910 to 1914 the *Wimbledon Borough News* carried accounts of Rose's regular talks, and also reports that on 15 June 1913, the day after Emily's London funeral procession, Rose was back holding yet another public meeting on the Common (*Wimbledon Borough News*, 14 June 1913, p. 2). The newspaper's brief mentions over a lengthy period of various names suggested that there had been much toing and froing between various members of the Wimbledon and Kensington WSPU branches, in particular by Barbara Wylie, a woman who had also been a WSPU organiser in Scotland; this interested us greatly for reasons discussed later. In addition it provided obituaries and led to the memoirs of other people who related more information about Rose, Gertrude and Harold.

In the *Wimbledon Borough News* of 26 March 1926 (p. 10) there was an obituary of Harold Baillie-Weaver, but no later one of Gertrude. The *News* reports that he was the chairman 'of the League of Peace and Freedom for the period of its existence'. This is a mistake, for the Women's International League for Peace and Freedom was a women-only organisation, but it does suggest that Harold as well as Gertrude was likely to have been noted for pacifist convictions (remember that Gertrude had been stoned in Saffron

Walden in 1914 for publicly expressing pacifist sentiments). The *Wimbledon and Merton News* of 12 November 1954, p. 10) contained an obituary of Rose Lamartine Yates, who had died a week earlier on 5 November (how appropriate of Rose to go out to fireworks!) aged seventy nine.

Rose's militant suffragism is recorded; she addressed meetings on Wimbledon Common every Sunday from 1910 to 1914 and dealt with hecklers in a witty fashion. I later found (MofL 57.113/12) that these meetings were held in defiance of government and police, as a principled defence of the right of free speech and free assembly. Rose organised the local WSPU shop and had the famous 'Votes for Women' soap manufactured for it; it became a soup kitchen during the First World War.[28] From 1919 to 1922 she was an independent member of the London County Council but didn't stand again because of the ill health of her husband Thomas (they were married in 1900 and he died in 1929). She was an active member of the Cyclists Touring Club, cycling all over Europe with Thomas from 1900 until she became involved in the WSPU in 1908.)

By luck and by dint of Ann's hobby of reading her way through library catalogues cross-referencing things, Wimbledon Library provided more information about both the Baillie-Weavers and also Rose. Lady Emily Lutyens' *Candles in the Sun* (1957, pp. 76–8) states that Harold was a barrister, 'married to a widow much older than himself' (p. 76) – coincidentally, Lady Emily was Con Lytton's youngest sister (Lytton, 1914, p. 293). In the spring of 1915 her two sons became friendly with Harold in Bude in Cornwall; he 'christened himself "Padre" . . . had been something of a beau in his day, and he helped to give both boys their great sartorial interest'. He wanted the two boys to live with him in his rooms in the Temple in London, but instead they lived with both Baillie-Weavers for a short time in a rented house in Wimbledon (this was Eastward Ho!, the house in which both Baillie-Weavers lived until Harold's death). However, the arrangement didn't work out, in part (according to Lady Emily) because all 'minor lapses' were greatly frowned on by one or both of the Baillie-Weavers. The boys were passed on to Lady De La Warr,[29] a Theosophical associate of the Baillie-Weavers, and through her to Annie Besant, at that time still a very active leader of the Theosophical Society of which Harold became secretary in 1916 and in which the Lutyens were also involved. And it was Lady De La Warr who had been instrumental in the house in Wimbledon being rented by the Baillie-Weavers.

It seems from this that it was theosophy (and Annie Besant?) that brought Gertrude to Wimbledon, and not the already existing feminist link with Rose Lamartine Yates. If so, it is still likely that the presence of Rose and an existing knowledge of a feminist community in Wimbledon added to its attractions for her.

Ann's cross-referencing also provided a much later glimpse of Rose Lamartine Yates, in Kathleen Fisher's *Sun and Shadows* (1982, pp. 57–8; and see also the photograph of Rose). Travelling to Germany in 1935, Kathleen Fisher's friend Violet – who had met Rose on her world tour in 1929 – arranged for Rose to travel with them to Munich. This brief account mentions that Rose had the return half of Emily Davison's railway ticket (it had in fact been in Emily's purse, which was one of her effects given to Thomas Yates when he represented Mrs Davison at the inquest held on Emily). It also says that Rose had dressed her son Paul as a girl for some years (Fisher, 1982, p. 57):

> . . . she was disappointed when she had a boy and not a girl. For some years she dressed him in girls' clothes and had a portrait in oils made with a purple sash across him which carried the slogan 'Down with Asquith'.

Rose also vehemently disapproved of Kathleen Fisher letting her husband register for her at a hotel: '"*You*," she told me, "should sign as Mrs Fisher and then write Mr Fisher underneath!"' (Fisher, 1982, p. 58).

We have no problems at all in seeing what it was that enabled Rose and Emily to get on so well.

A small brown tin trunk

The *Wimbledon Borough News* obituary of Rose contained what was at the time a complete stunner. In 1929 Rose returned from a world tour to 'start a unique collection of documents and insignia relating to the Women's Suffrage Movement, collected funds and opened the "Women's Record House" at her new home in Great Smith Street . . . then this was destroyed by bombing during the

1939–1945 war'. Just *what* was in it? And how much of it related to Emily? We knew that Emily's remaining possessions given to the Fawcett Library by Ruth Yates in 1986 originally came from Rose Lamartine Yates. Were these too precious, too private a reminder of her dead friend to go in the Women's Record House collection? We didn't know at the time, but we would both have given a great deal to have been able to spend a day or so there the week before that bombing took place.

The answer to a maiden's prayer does not often come in the shape of a small, battered, brown tin trunk. When I finally managed to take up the Fawcett Library's very generous offer to work on the still uncatalogued 'Emily Wilding Davison papers' I found that they reside in a small trunk. They are perhaps misnamed, for at least some of them are the remains of the contents of the Women's Record House. *Were* the contents destroyed in the Second World War? According to a Suffragette Fellowship newsletter of 1939–40 (MofL 73.83/59 (c)), the records 'have been removed to a place of safety' (p. 2). Many items still have the card in Rose's neat handwriting recording who gave them and what their significance is. The trunk also contained a faded Madonna lily carried at Emily's funeral procession, a note on toilet paper smuggled out of Holloway in someone's shoe, notices concerning the Suffragette Fellowship, a WSPU calling card of February 1913 with the signatures of Emmeline Pethick-Lawrence, Rose Lamartine Yates and Maria Tyson on the back[30] (what *had* they been up to?), together with Emily Davison's letters, essays, papers, her book of press cuttings and mementoes.

Many of Emily Davison's own papers are incredibly sad to hold, to touch. There is the letter from her mother written as she lay dying, conveying unbearable anguish; her racing card for Derby Day with all the races up to the fateful 3 p.m. race marked with her fancies; her helper's pass card for the WSPU Summer Festival at the Empress Rooms in Kensington for 2.30–10.30 p.m. that day. It was strange to think how few people had seen and held these things since Emily had done so. The papers provided the answers to some questions, half-answers to a few more, and some new puzzles. I discuss what they tell us of Emily's socialism and feminism in the Militancy chapter; here I focus on the web of friendship itself.

A number of names appear of women who played some important role in Emily Davison's life. For some months in 1913 (at least from February to May) she lived at the home of a Mrs Green at 133 Clapham Road – *The Suffragette* of 13 June 1913 had noted a Mrs Green among the visitors to Emily's bedside in Epsom. Emily collected many press cuttings of letters sent to newspapers by Mrs Eugenie Freeman and by E.M. Clarke (the Miss Clarke mentioned in the Colmore biography?), as well as by herself. She kept in contact with Katherine Riddell of Rubislaw Den South in Aberdeen, whose address she gave in December 1912 when arrested for assaulting the Baptist minister mistaken for Lloyd George.[31] Katherine Gillett Gatty,[32] who was later active in the Suffragette Fellowship and in this context wrote warmly of Emily (letter 31 August 1937 from KGG, Emily Davison papers, Fawcett Library), invited her to tea on 28 May 1913.

Someone called Lil or Let or Liet (the writing is very difficult to decipher), who signs herself Emily's loving sister, in an undated letter with no address says that life is not a bed of roses with Fred, especially now that the baby has come. Emily had no sister or half-sister with a name anything like this – so is this perhaps the wife of her brother Alfred? This letter also says that Emily's sweets have been sent to Clapham (presumably to 133 Clapham Road), and that in case there aren't enough boxes she is not to tell . . . Just who I will say in its proper place.

However, more than anything else these papers confirm the importance of Rose Lamartine Yates, Elinor Penn Gaskell and Mary Leigh for Emily Davison. All three of these women, with Mrs Green, telegraphed to Emily's mother telling her of the Derby incident. Rose also wrote to her with what encouraging news she could, then telling her of Emily's death. Mrs Davison wrote to Rose in 1914 (Mrs Davison to RLY, 2 June 1914, Emily Davison papers, Fawcett Library) thanking her for her sympathy concerning her 'dear daughter's sacrifice' and asking her to thank Thomas

> . . . for his letter and the Daily Sketch May 28th containing that beautiful message from dear Emily . . . I feel most grateful to your husband for all he has done for me & send him my sincere thanks.

It thus seems plausible that it was Thomas and Rose who arranged the publication of 'The price of liberty', who were determined that Emily should not be forgotten on the anniversary of her death in spite of the leadership of the WSPU. It was also Rose and Thomas who put up Captain Henry Davison (he lived in Ashton in Bexhill) in Wimbledon during the inquest and funeral procession in London (Captain Davison to TLY, 20 June 1913, Emily Davison papers, Fawcett Library.

It is not surprising that the prepondrance of material here should concern Rose, given its origin; it does not necessarily mean she was more important to Emily than other people whose letters appear here (or indeed, as I discuss later, those of whom almost nothing is said). Certainly Elinor Penn Gaskell must have been greatly trusted by Emily. The papers contain two copies of 'The price of liberty'; one, much corrected, appears loose; the other, perfectly typed, is inside an envelope whose postdate is unreadable but which is addressed c/o Mrs Penn Gaskell in Kilburn.

Perhaps the trunk's most significant indication of loving friendship is a small green book, a selection of Walt Whitman poems. From a quotation on the title page the words 'the institution of the dear love of comrades' are underscored; beneath this 'from Comrade Davison/to Comrade Leigh' and the date, 29 December 1912. Inside some passages are marked by the same pencilled hand: 'I hear it is charged against me that I seek to destroy institutions', 'I dreamed a city of friends', and others that are more personal; all speak to the dear love of comrades.

Establishing the precise whereabouts of Emily Davison and Mary Leigh from late December 1912 to the middle of January 1913 has proved very difficult. Emily moved around the country on WSPU and militant business, was imprisoned in Aberdeen on 30 November 1912 and released, very ill, on 4 December; then within days she engaged in a long series, throughout December and January, of speaking and other engagements in the north and north-west (including in Manchester, Newcastle and Morpeth). During this time Mary Leigh was under virtual house arrest in Dublin following her release from prison after a long period of forcible feeding and consequent fears for her life. Thus a meeting between the two of them in December 1912 or January 1913 is unlikely, if not impossible. Of course, Emily could have posted the book to Mary Leigh; but then there is a need to explain how and why Mary Leigh gave it to Rose and the Women's Record House – especially given Mary's ferocious and proven loyalty to comrades and her longstanding refusal to open up her private self to public feminist scrutiny. I think the book was never given, and was among Emily's possessions that Thomas and Rose Lamartine Yates took after her death.

However, having earlier worked on letters from feminist friends and from many lesbian women to Edward Carpenter in the Carpenter Collection,[33] I wondered whether an educated, reading and thinking woman like Emily could have not known the sexual-political significance of such a gift, tantamount in many circles to a declaration of sexual love expressed through the words and phrases of Whitman. With this in mind I was interested to read in Emily's 'Incendiarism' essay, concerning her decision to set fire to pillar boxes as a militant protest, that her 'good friend and comrade arrived to take charge of me' when she returned from remand to the court hearing on 21 December 1911, and of Emily's great pleasure at her arrival. After the decision to release Emily on bail pending trial in January 1912 at Assizes, the many suffragette friends who had crowded the court left to have lunch elsewhere, 'leaving me to eat mine with my faithful friend' while she waited for bail to be arranged. And later in the same essay she says that 'After a joyous celebration I went off for two nights with one of my comrades' before going to Longhorsley to see her mother, rightly anticipating a long sentence at her January trial. However, Mary Leigh was in prison in Holloway for window breaking from early December until 23 January and could not have been she (*VFW*, 1 December 1911, p. 144) – the identity of this 'faithful friend and comrade' whose arrival was so pleasing and whose presence was so comforting remains unknown.

On balance, after considering this incident and the gift of the Whitman poems, I concluded that Emily used the notion of the 'dear love of comrades' with nothing other than political comradeship in mind. But then again . . .

'A loving Aberdeen friend'

Our – somewhat different – political and emotional responses to the Emily Davison that we began to piece together changed a good deal over the course of producing this book, as may easily be imagined. But although some of her behaviour can now be more easily understood, in particular her acts of militancy, in other respects we are no further forward than when we started. Neither of us can decide whether we would like Emily Davison if ever time travel or other means should enable us to meet. Although we have somewhat different reasons for this, it is interesting that the basis of the undecidedness is the same: the pronounced lack of 'human interest' material on Emily Davison the woman. What was she *like*? This still largely eludes us.

In some ways the most interesting things we know about Emily are apparently trivial. She was so excited on hearing she had got her degree that she emptied the local shop of 'black bullets' to distribute to Longhorsley children. She liked cats (see Colmore, 1913, p. 50; Lytton, 1914, p. 209). She liked musical comedy and she left the sheet music for 'The Policeman's Holiday' at a friend's house in Longhorsley when she returned to London in April/May 1913. She didn't mind being teased by local Morpeth and Longhorsley people about her feminism.

Emily's unpublished essays and published reviews also reveal her as a thinking woman, one who tried to face life's complexities, to puzzle out moral and ethical questions and dilemmas, and who tried very hard to be a truly caring and responsible person. Emily was tall and her hair was a reddish dark blond. She had a habit of putting her head on one side and smiling quizzically; her expression was mobile and she photographed badly, for photographs made her seem stiff and solemn in a way she wasn't in life. She seems to have been an 'attractive' woman, whose personality, although rather overawing, also endeared her to people. Her total commitment to the feminist cause, a complete conviction that right was on her side and a certain bookishness were combined with a sense of humour; she was exuberant on occasion, and not ashamed of 'common' and 'unintellectual' tastes.

This is a real woman, someone contradictory, complex, 'caught' and, like most of us, truly seen only in what appear to be inconsequentialities, trivialities. To drag the myth and the woman apart and begin to distinguish between them is to understand more about why the woman acted as she did. The main way we have come closer to Emily has been by tracking down her friends and comrades in the feminist cause. In our search for the women already referred to, we stumbled on another, whose existence has been almost obliterated and appears in no other published source. It is clear to us that she was very close to Emily indeed, perhaps closer than any of the women discussed so far, including the deeply admired Mary Leigh.[34]

This part of the story of Emily Davison's friendships began with Ann reading contemporary copies of the local Newcastle and Morpeth newspapers in Newcastle Library. The *Illustrated Chronicle* of 16 June 1913 was the most important, since it had four pages of photographs and several pages of text coverage of the London procession and Morpeth funeral. What caught Ann's attention was the report that a marble open book, carved with the words 'Emily Wilding Davison, Oct 1872 – June 1913' on one page and on the other 'A veritable princess of spirituality. From a loving Aberdeen friend', had been carried beside the driver of the hearse with Emily's coffin.

There was no mention of any Aberdeen friend in the Colmore biography, and nor had our research into Emily's friends uncovered an Aberdeen connection, so this was intriguing in the extreme. At this time other information in the same *Illustrated Chronicle* about family members at the actual funeral ceremony in Morpeth escaped our serious attention, although we did notice that the first carriage contained not only Emily's closest family members but also a Miss Morrison who was the 'companion of late Miss Davison'. The obvious question was 'what companion?' However, our attention was focused on finding out about the 'loving Aberdeen friend'. Ann's inquiries about the Aberdeen friend among various north-eastern contacts produced nothing, but more casual inquiries about Miss Morrison did: it was suggested that she might be a friend of Emily's father, Charles, who had witnessed his will before his death in 1893 (this later turned out not to be so, as his will shows). However, we rather wondered if she might be the friend of Emily's mother that *The Times* (9 June 1913, p. 8) says stayed many hours at Emily's bedside as she lay dying. Miss Morrison didn't seem very interesting to us but the 'loving Aberdeen friend' certainly did.

Inquiries to Morpeth stonemasons and funeral directors produced nothing other than that the hearse drapes had been kept by the undertaker for many years and were used as blackout material in the Second World War, while the horses' plumes had been destroyed only a short time before (to Ann's great disappointment). The search for Charles Davison's will never seemed to progress, as we waited week after endless week for copies of this and others to arrive from Somerset House; an attempt to find the 'mother's friend' was equally unsuccessful.

However, what had not occurred to either of us was that Miss

Morrison might be a suffragette herself: we had imagined her aged sixty or seventy or perhaps even older at the time of Emily's death. Then later one night as I was reading photocopies of *The Suffragette*, in an article on 'The militant movement in 1913' I found a brief mention of the trial of 'Dr Chalmers Smith and Miss Margaret Morrison of Glasgow', which took place around October 1913 (*The Suffragette*, 2 January 1914, p. 276). A *Scottish* Miss Morrison, a *feminist* Miss Morrison! With great excitement we visited Manchester Central Reference Library which holds a complete set of *The Suffragette* on microfilm, and consulted the complete set of *Votes For Women* in the University of York Morrell Library. We noted with amusement that first Dorothea Chalmers Smith and then Margaret Morrison managed to escape from custody (*VFW*, 28 November 1913, p. 131). Mentions of Miss M. Morrison as a speaker, making contributions to funds and so forth, were painstakingly collected; but no connection with Aberdeen was found, only a longstanding one with Glasgow. Knowing that it wasn't good enough to think, 'Well, it's in Scotland, it's not far', we pursued Miss Morrison further, mention by brief mention. Soon we came across other Morrisons (and later they multiplied into seven or eight, like dopplegangers haunting all our waking and some of our sleeping hours); the other main one was a Mrs Mary, Australian half-sister of Gilbert Murray and a stalwart of the St John's Wood and Kensington WSPUS.

During our search the heading 'Aberdeen Women's Suffrage Association' caught my eye. And there she was, a Miss E.J.D. Morrison, vice-president of the Aberdeen WSA in June 1908 (*VFW*, 25 June 1908, p. 271). How fast the heart can beat without bursting! Miss Morrison was at Mairchel College; the Aberdeen Association was mixed and active. There was great excitement in the library at this point but also some cursing, for we had not been working on the issues year by consecutive year (there is a lesson to be learnt from this). So, starting again, we pursued *this* Miss Morrison.

There was another surprise in store. We were now looking for her in Aberdeen, whereas we next found her in Kensington in 1910 (*VFW*, 14 January 1910, p. 261). In a brief report of London and 'round the country' WSPU groups, Evelyn Sharp is named as the Kensington WSPU organiser and Miss E. Morrison speaks at an election meeting. More excitement, more careful searching ensued.

In April 1909 Miss E. Morrison was an active member of the

WSPU branch in Aberdeen, at a time when Adela Pankhurst was the paid organiser there, according to a report by Adela herself (*VFW*, 2 April 1909, p. 511). (Adela, like Sylvia Pankhurst, was 'banished' as soon as possible it seems.) In the same issue of *Votes For Women* (p. 506), Emily is mentioned being arrested yet again. Two months later, Miss E. Morrison is active in the Kensington branch, speaking at Monmouth Road in Kensington (*VFW*, 28 June 1909, p. 846). We concluded that she must have moved from Aberdeen following her finals, probably in the second or third week in June, and that she must have been very involved to re-commence political work so soon.

A high level of activity by this Miss Morrison follows. She was speaking at about two meetings a week according to *Votes For Women* of 11 February 1910 (p. 312), and then becomes the joint honorary secretary of the Kensington WSPU with Louisa Eates (*VFW*, 18 February 1910, p. 327). Miss Morrison was elected at the branch AGM at which Miss Brackenbury (probably Georgina, the elder of the two militant and artist Brackenbury sisters) and Miss Wylie joined the committee. Barbara Wylie was one of the Kensington members who often went to the Wimbledon WSPU; an ex-WSPU Scottish organiser, she was also a frequent visitor to Scottish WSPU branches – including Aberdeen, when the WSPU group there appeared to fold after 1910.

Even reading microfilm carefully, it's almost impossible not to miss things. A chance re-reading by Ann of issues for 1909 filled another gap in our information that was infuriating both of us: her name. 'E.J.D.' was just not enough: another Emily, we pondered; not Edith, we hoped; possibly Emma, or Elizabeth . . .

A somewhat different style of group report appeared in *Votes For Women* of 17 September 1909 (p. 1190) which used first names instead of initials:

> The speakers at our weekly At Home next Tuesday evening, September 21 . . . will be Miss Evelyn Morrison, BA, and Mr Laurence Housman. Everyone will be welcome.

So it was Evelyn.

Votes For Women of 15 July 1910 (p. 681) gives the plans for marshalling at the forthcoming WSPU Hyde Park demonstration. Miss E. Morrison was to act as a 'group captain' in the West Procession under 'General' Drummond in Section B, group B2.

This was the closest we spotted her and Emily: even so, two women among a crowd of anything up to 200,000 can't really count as 'close'!

The next couple of years of *Votes For Women* included many mentions of Miss Morrison working away in the Kensington area, at branch meetings and also at many public meeting. Longstanding member though she was, she does not seem to have engaged in overtly militant work – as far as can be seen from lists of prisoners, she was never imprisoned in the militant cause. In this she is much more typical of wspu members than any of Emily Davison's other friends or, indeed, than Emily herself. Around 1911 she seems to have become less active. For instance, it seems that she gave up the secretaryship to a Miss Postlethwaite around 1911, but on later occasions and as favours she would chair particular meetings.

We found no concrete evidence, then, of a link between Evelyn Morrison and Emily Davison. What we had was indirect and circumstantial evidence that E.J.D. Morrison of Aberdeen was Evelyn Morrison of London and that she was probably the 'loving Aberdeen friend'.[35] But there remained the newspaper report of the funeral in Morpeth and the open book with its public statement of strong affection that was placed on Emily's grave. Let us consider this in more detail.

Edwardian funerals, even of suffragettes, were very formal affairs; what was considered right and proper was done. Emily Wilding Davison's actual funeral, as distinct from all the marches and processions with guards and banners that accompanied it both in London and in Morpeth, was a distinctly family affair. All the paraphernalia of the suffragette martyr's death stopped outside the church grounds in Morpeth, according to both the *Morpeth Herald and Chronicle* (20 June 1913, p. 2) and the *Illustrated Chronicle*. The *Chronicle* states that the procession stopped at the lychgate, and only after the family funeral was over and the family had gone did suffragettes enter to drop flowers on the grave: 'The proceedings in the church at Morpeth were private, the congregation being restricted as far as possible to relatives' (16 June 1913, p. 2).

Moreover, on the same page of the *Chronicle* the order of relatives in their respective carriages is given: the best possible guide as to who was seen to have the greatest social/emotional claims on the remains of Emily Davison. In the first carriage were:

Mrs Davison (mother), Madame de Becker, of St Malo, France (sister), Mrs Lewis Bilton, Darlington (Cousin), and Miss Morrison, London (companion of late Miss Davison)

And Miss Morrison's marble book (for we were assuming that she was indeed the 'loving Aberdeen friend': the coincidence was too great to suggest otherwise) was carried in full public view on the hearse and its 'remarkable emblem' was reported in full in the wondering press (*Illustrated Chronicle*, 16 June 1913, p. 10).

Miss Morrison's claims to Emily were thus recognised publicly by Mrs Davison. If Emily's mother, the chief mourner, hadn't sanctioned her presence, there is no way that she would have been allowed anywhere near the first carriage. Of course, it is still possible that Miss Morrison was a family connection – but all connections are acknowleged in the local newspapers. We concluded that she wasn't related, but that her relationship with Emily Davison was not only very close but also accepted by Emily's mother.

It is entirely possible that she was a friend of Mrs Davison's, that Mrs Davison knew and liked her; and that as well as being Emily's 'companion' (according to the *Morpeth Herald and Reporter* of 20 June 1913, p. 3, her 'intimate companion') Mrs Davison counted her as a friend. It is also possible that it was she who stayed at Emily's bedside and was described by *The Times* as a friend of Emily's mother rather than of Emily's: she might have used that description to stay at Emily's bedside. These things are possible, but we don't have any evidence about them.

After piecing together the above, we scrutinised the photograph of the chief mourners that appears in the *Illustrated Chronicle* (16 June 1913, p. 9) with new interest. Four *women* are clearly visible at the head of the group, although their faces are heavily veiled – and how fitting that this should be so at Emily's funeral. The first two must be Mrs Davison supported by Emily's half-sister, Mme de Becker.[36] The second two must be the cousin Mrs Bilton and Miss Morrison, but which of them is which? Is Miss Morrison the woman with deeply bowed head carrying a basket of flowers to strew on the coffin?

How did they become friends? One possibility is that Emily Davison met Miss Morrison during wspu work the former did in Scotland, and their friendship was a planned or an accidental consequence of Miss Morrison's move to London. Another is that Emily didn't meet her until after Miss Morrison moved to Kensington in June 1909. We calculated that if Miss Morrison went to university at the 'usual' age of eighteen, after graduation in 1909 she would have been twenty-one or twenty-two, while Emily was thirty-six. But of course many women, both then and now, are considerably older when they go to college or university, so she might have been much closer to Emily's own age. At this point Ann went to Kensington Public Library and both of us considered the Evelyn Sharp papers in the Bodleian Library in Oxford, with consequences I outline later.

At this point, we knew pitifully little about Miss Morrison. What kind of a woman was she? What did she do for a living? How had she come to know Emily? What happened to her after 1913? Had she known what Emily was going to do and what had she thought about it? These and many more questions ran through both our minds and were the topic of much conversation between us. I sent off a letter to Aberdeen University and thought that perhaps either *The Vote* or the Women's International League for Peace and Freedom (the international feminist pacifist organisation) might provide more information, but came up with precisely nothing. After one completely sleepless night, Ann went back to Manchester Central Reference Library and to basics: the British Library catalogue and other indices. And, *miribile dictu*, wonderful to relate:

An E.J.D. Morrison wrote a pamphlet that was indexed in the British Library catalogue; it was on the history of the village of Claverton and was published by the Claverton Down Women's Institute in 1964. Claverton Down is in Bath. The records of the Claverton Down wi were deposited in Bath Local History Library in 1986; the Librarian thought we might not be interested: there were just a few letters to Miss Morrison (ah, this E.J.D.*was* a woman then: we hadn't been sure with the use of initials only) and, oh yes, a photograph of her. The next day at dawn we set off. From the library we went to people who had been neighbours while she was alive and to wi colleagues.

The pamphlet had originated in a piece entitled 'The Story of Claverton in the County of Somerset', which had won a national wi prize. In its time it was requested by libraries and antiquarian societies and other 'learned' sources from all over the world, including the Library of Congress. It is still reckoned to be one of the best local histories and its use of primary sources dating back to the medieval period is meticulous. Although nominally 'edited' by her, it was in fact Miss Morrison who did the research, wrote and typed it. Neighbours remember Miss Morrison and her sister Aileen typing all night while it was being written.

The Claverton wi was started in 1948. According to the local Kelly's Directories, Miss Morrison came to Bath in about 1952. She has earlier worked for the Ministry of Health. Her sister Aileen and she lived together; both were active in the wi. At least two of the Morrison girls (there was another sister who married, and possibly a brother) became barristers and had been called to the Bar. Miss Morrison herself had been one of the first women silks.

The photograph of Miss Morrison was 'not as we knew her but the only one her brother thought suitable', as is noted on the back. In it she is posed as a Portia in a barrister's wig, a young judge with thoughtful hand on thoughtful chin purposefully staring with calm eyes out of the picture. Indeed she seems to us just the kind of woman that Emily Davison would have liked, admired, been close to. Her name, however, was *Edith*, Edith Jane Douglas Morrison. Our conclusion at the time was that the new hand penning notices about the Kensington wspu had perhaps confused Evelyn Sharp the organiser and Edith Morrison the joint secretary.

Edith Morrison gave up being a practising barrister because to succeed would have required her to shout down other people; none the less everyone who had known her still referred to her as 'Miss Morrison the lady barrister' – a puzzle at the time. She was slight and not very tall; in later years she had great character lines on her face. Usually quietly assured, she could make a fuss when necessary. Aileen was more reserved and more obviously 'the lady' than Edith, who was a definite 'presence'. Both sisters had unmistakable Irish accents (we translated this into 'posh Scottish' to explain people's 'mistake'). It was Edith who was the motor force of their outside involvements. Interestingly, her sister is referred to as Aileen, Edith always as 'Miss Morrison' by those who knew them.

Both sisters had been involved with the wi and were Friends of the local long-stay hospital, Edith more actively so. Edith had given a talk on bbc Radio's 'Woman's Hour' about her time as a suffragette in the wspu. She had also been an active member of the local Council for Social Service and involved in what later became

Age Concern. When in her seventies, she was often invited by various organisations to give a talk on ageing and old age (a very moving talk, a typescript of which we were sent by a former css colleague). Both friends and neighbours remarked that Miss Morrison was not the kind of women to suffer silliness or undue romantics, nor had she any wish for notoriety for its own sake – just the kind of woman to believe in doing what one believed in for its own sake only.

Around 1962 Edith and Aileen sold their house and moved into separate hotels in Bath that then specialised in caring for the elderly. Edith Morrison died in July 1964 at the age of eighty-one (*Bath and Wilts Evening Chronicle*, 17 July 1964, p. 18; *Bath Weekly Chronicle*, 18 July 1964, p. 29), some time after suffering a bad fall. Her sister Aileen lived until 1968. The brief report of Edith Morrison's fall and hospitalisation (*Bath and Wilts Evening Chronicle*, 21 June 1964, p. 5) merely noted that she had been a former suffragette. The notices of her death said 'Funeral private. No flowers'. How very unlike the death and funeral of Emily Davison.

This was the sum of what we discovered via the Bath connection about Edith Morrison the friend of Emily Davison. The librarian at Broadcasting House was unable to trace the recording of her 'Woman's Hour' talk, and a reading of ten years' issues of the *Radio Times* failed to find a mention of it. However, a few days after our third visit to Bath, a letter arrived from the archivist at Aberdeen University which filled in some of the gaps, but also provided us with some new ones. Edith Morrison was indeed Irish, having been born in November 1883 in Londonderry. Her father was the Reverend Hugh Morrison, who later had a living as a United Free minister in Cults, in Aberdeen. She lived in the family manse while a student at Aberdeen University from 1905 to 1909, taking English (a prize), history and political economy as subsidiaries and natural philosophy – that is, physics – and mathematics as her honours. In 1909 she left Aberdeen, but not for London: for a post teaching science at St Bride's School in Edinburgh.

This was a bombshell for us, for it was conclusive evidence that the Miss E. Morrison active in Kensington from June 1909 on was not Edith at all. If it was needed, Ann then found a further confirmation in the pages of the *Kensington Times* (24 September 1909, p. 2). The Misses Brackenbury held an 'At Home' at which

> Miss Evelyn Morrison, BA . . . dealt with 'The Women's Vote in Australia and New Zealand', a subject on which she is well qualified to speak as being a native of Australia . . .

The Miss E. Morrison who was joint secretary at Kensington was indeed an Evelyn then; the same newspaper showed that she was the daughter of the Mrs Mary Morrison referred to earlier.

We then began to put together small pieces of information about the 'real' Miss Morrison, Edith. Another re-reading of *The Vote* produced the information that Edith was taking some Bar examinations in 1922 (*The Vote*, 20 January 1922, p. 18; 9 November 1923, p. 355) and was among the first twenty-four women barristers, being called to the Bar on 19 November 1923 (*The Vote*, 23 November 1923, p. 371). This last was coupled with the interesting information that at the time Edith was an inspector in the Insurance Department of the Ministry of Health (*The Vote* contains much information about this Ministry over the years, suggesting that many feminist women worked for it). Unfortunately the records of Gray's Inn, where Miss Morrison was called to the Bar, were destroyed during the Second World War, so we have found nothing else concerning her legal career. The absence of her name from lists of barristers and their chambers suggests she never practised. But between 1923 and 1953 Edith Morrison disappears from view: what was she doing until she retired?

Thus far we had found *nothing* that connected Edith Morrison and Emily Davison other than the Morpeth funeral and the marble book. We had become reconciled to this, recognising just how private a person Edith had been, when an unexpected bonus later rewarded us for all our thwarted research. In the Fawcett Library, reading through Emily Davison's essays and letters, I could barely believe it when I read, in the undated letter from her 'loving sister' Lil or Let or Liet earlier referred to, that

> Your sweets have been sent to Clapham: *Don't tell* the Morrisons as I don't think I've enough boxes.

Still not conclusive proof (it could be those wretched Australian Morrison's who had so confused us before), but the closest yet. According to the lists of subscribers to *The Suffragette*, the Misses Morrison (Edith and Aileen are the only Morrison sisters we have found) contributed to funds in 1912 and subscribed in 1913 and then again in 1914 (*VFW*, 31 May 1921, p. 556; WSPU Seventh Annual Report, 1913; WSPU Eighth Annual Report, 1914).

Those unfamiliar with the Women's Institute, or who know it only through BBC radio soap operas, may think of it as cosy gatherings of middle-class women concerned only with home-made jam and harvest homes. There is nothing wrong with such gatherings, but in fact the history of the WI in this country is that of active, vocal and politically aware women, who not only met together *as women* during the 1940s and 1950s, when no other local 'women's groups' existed, but also organised together to act, to reform, to change. Precisely all the kinds of things that the many Portias involved in the WSPU believed in and cared about. Of the other women already mentioned, Vera Holme and Louisa Eates both became involved in the WI in later years. We wonder just how many other feminists did so in the period after 1919, and suspect there were a good many. We were delighted that in her retirement Edith Morrison still gave her allegiance to women, to women organising together.

As for Edith Morrison herself, in some ways we feel we know her better than any of these other women, Emily Davison included. We have talked to people who knew her well and worked with her in various voluntary organisations, seen the look in their eyes, heard the tone of their voices when they spoke of her. A very private woman, one who worked behind the scenes, but an entirely principled woman as well. Edith Morrison was kind, warm-hearted, redoubtable, tough, and deeply caring of others – a thoroughly nice woman, indeed a remarkable one, but also of some mystery who continues to intrigue us.

Somewhat late in our researches we realised the extent to which WSPU women tended to use aliases containing parts of their real names. Having casually noted the existence of an active Jane Douglas, we now wonder if this might have been an alias of Edith Morrison. And we are also perplexed by the fact that after the public statement of the marble book on Emily's grave Mary Leigh, and not Edith Morrison, kept both the grave and the marble book in good order for half a century. We continue to look for answers to these two puzzles, but, as this book went to press, we found the answer to another. It seems that Edith Morrison spent some years working in Stoke-on-Trent in a legal capacity, for in her will she requested that a present from the North Stafford Law Students

Society should be cremated with her (and her ashes scattered in Trentham Park in Stoke). Thus, although she was never a practising barrister, it is likely that she had a legal career which included some teaching.

5
Militancy: 'Doing Something Silly' instead of 'Doing Something Cruel'

The mere idea of militancy

The mere idea of WSPU militancy still has the ability to rouse powerful and negative emotions in people. How strange this is, after eighty years and the deaths of only four suffragettes.[37] There is something about the militant action of *women*, no matter how relatively mild it is, that disturbs and, yes, annoys and rankles, in a way that the much more violent and destructive militancy of men in other radical groups does not. For instance, there are interesting differences in reaction of the media and academics to female and male members of the Baeder-Meinhoff gang: the activities of the women are seen as the product of sexual hang-ups about men in general or of unresolved Oedipal complexes concerning their fathers, while the men are seen as politically motivated revolutionaries. Radical women, almost by definition, are seen as having sexual hang-ups; radical men are radical men. Be that as it may, a strong case against militancy, on the grounds of political tactics as well as opposition to violence, has been made in some detail by various commentators (including Fulford, 1957; Rosen, 1974; Mitchell, 1977) and in passing by others, for example notably by Holton (1980, 1987).

In this chapter I focus on two previously under-discussed aspects of feminist militancy. The first is the way acts of militancy took place in the context of personal friendship and worries about what was happening to particular feminist women, rather than in relation to the tactical dictates of Christabel Pankhurst or any other member of the WSPU leadership. The second is the way the police and press presented militant acts to the public (the ubiquitous 'man in the street': the public is never a woman, we should note) in a form unrecognisable to the women supposedly responsible for them. The discussion begins with Mary Leigh who, with Emily Davison and Charlotte Marsh, was described as one of the 'saints of the Church Militant' by Mrs Pethick-Lawrence (*VFW*, 15 October 1909, p. 8).

I have already noted that Mary Leigh's account of her action in the 'hatchet' case of 1909 was significantly different from the police account, according to which she had flung a real rather than a toy hatchet without heed and so had seriously wounded Redmond's head.[38] Since public knowledge of the case was derived third-hand from newspapers or from being told stories gleaned by other people who took them from newspapers, it was the police view that prevailed, for this was what the non-feminist press reported.

Similarly, when Mary Leigh and Charlotte Marsh occupied a roof-top and threw slates down near the hall where Asquith was speaking in Birmingham in September the same year, what was reported was a vision of slates hurtling into the Asquith carriage. As Margot Asquith suggested, reality was rather different (Mitchell, 1977, p. 145). She wrote to Herbert Gladstone, then Home Secretary, to say that hard labour was too severe a sentence, for not one of the slates went anywhere near either herself or her husband. Then as now, reality was often just too tame for many newspapers – and it was not clear-cut enough for many of the police officers involved in administering the state response to militancy.

This pattern of exaggerated misrepresentation of militant acts can be discerned with the so-called secret arson campaign that took place from the spring of 1913 to the summer of 1914, supposedly set in motion by Emily Davison setting fire to pillar-boxes in December 1912.

Certainly, through the spring and summer of 1913, Christabel Pankhurst in various editorials in *The Suffragette* extolled the benefits of a secret arson campaign to be carried out regardless of the hardships that might be caused by, for example, the destruction of letters containing postal orders for poor women. Secret arson attacks on some properties were carried out by WSPU arsonists with orders from the leadership,[39] which effectively took responsibility for them by printing details of the attacks in *The Suffragette*, now under tight leadership control.

But those of us who are living through times in which sometimes three and four groups claim responsibility for acts of political terrorism should know that a claim for responsibility and actual responsibility are not always synonymous. In this respect, Mary Leigh's interview with David Mitchell (1977, p. 241) is instructive. She suggested that it was often the owners of property who carefully placed suffragette literature on the site of fires so as to claim insurance money and avoid being seen as responsible for having started the fires themselves. To this I would add that arsonists are not always politically or even financially motivated. Some people just like starting fires, and during this period they could do so with something like impunity – the police were more concerned to arrest suffragettes than to find the arsonist.

The proper conclusion to draw from this is that it is as necessary to subject official and press accounts of feminism and feminists to critical inquiry in the period of Emily Davison's life and death as it is now. This, of course, is something which people involved in any radical or 'marginal' organisation or activity will know is sensible: misrepresentation of feminists, of lesbians and gay men, of 'the left', and even of sociologists, are only too familiar to those of us who belong to any or all of these categories. However, recent historians of the suffragette movement have not been 'marginal' in this way. If they had been they might have been willing to dig beneath the official surface and also better able to 'see' and accept what is said about official versions of 'truth' by people whose lives and actions are treated as marginal in such accounts.

So, the 'case against militancy' by and large sees it in the terms set by the police and press (including, as noted, the WSPU newspaper itself after spring 1913). The case centres on two claims, which sometimes appear together and sometimes separately.

One claim, the simplest and in many ways the most convincing, is that militancy entailed violence and that recourse to violence by the WSPU not only 'spoilt' suffragette claims in the eyes of the public and the government, but also went against previously held moral and ethical principles. This is supported by a number of pieces of evidence. There is the alienation of the National Union of Women's Suffrage Societies (NUWSS) after a honeymoon period with the WSPU that lasted from 1906 to the start of 'violent' militancy in 1912. After this it is suggested that large numbers of women left the WSPU for the NUWSS, particularly in the wake of the arson campaign. There is the much earlier departure of WFL members, who were militant in their own way (with tax evasion and similar activities) but who eschewed the WSPU version of it. And, often produced as the *pièce de résistance*, there is the death of Emily Wilding Davison: her action hurt horse and jockey (we know which of the two many people seem to be most concerned about) and could have killed both.[40]

The other claim is the argument that the WSPU leadership, Christabel Pankhurst in particular, badly misread the political runes at the point when the best tactics would have been either to harness general public approbation of the suffragette cause or to engage in 'serious' arson against factories and railway lines (see Rosen, 1973, pp 214–45, for a plausible discussion of the latter). Christabel had a heady conviction of her own political and tactical infallibility, and she also faced a WSPU membership that applauded and followed the freelance arson of Emily Davison; this argument concludes that by institutionalising militancy Christabel Pankhurst not only made an 'immoral' decision, but also spoilt things by alienating members of the government otherwise sympathetic to the feminist cause at precisely the point when careful behind-the-scenes activity by the NUWSS was beginning to pay real dividends. These claims deserve scrutiny.

Militancy was not seen as violence by the vast majority of the women involved in it. For example, Emmeline Pethick-Lawrence (*VFW* 8 March 1908, p. 82) said, in response to the remark that women chaining themselves to railings was 'silly', that

> Doing something silly is the women's alternative to doing something cruel. The effect is the same. We use no violence because we can win freedom without it; because we have discovered an alternative.

Moreover, as many suffragettes emphasised over and over, the violence that ensued lay entirely in the *response* to feminist non-violent action such as sending deputations to Parliament, street speaking and the like. One interesting discussion of these issues has already been mentioned: Elinor Penn Gaskell pointed out that women's claims were justified and the action they wanted to take was perfectly reasonable; what was unjustified and unreasonable were the reactions of men (who often seized the opportunity to punch and kick and claw and also to sexually assault with impunity).

However, this was no good reason for women to stop, otherwise no political or religious or any other freedom would have been won in the past or would be won in the future. It is interesting that in criticisms of violence it is the wspu women who are effectively blamed for men's violence towards them. This is tantamount to blaming, for instance, Gandhi and other Indian pacifists for the violence and slaughter that their non-violent objections to racism and colonialism often occasioned.

However, it is true that later supposedly 'violent' means of militant protest were engaged in, stone-throwing being the first. The decision to eschew deputations and the like in favour of stone-throwing was a result of 'Black Friday', 18 November 1910, and of other incidents when protesting women were met with incredible violence and sexual assault by the police and the public – that is, by *men*. Much better to be arrested quickly after the throwing of a stone or two at a window or car than brave sexual and physical assault of the kind that had led to many injuries and at least three known deaths following Black Friday. However, self-protection was not the motive of the women who initiated this new form of militancy.

The day after Black Friday, Mary Leigh and Edith New went to Downing Street and lobbed stones at the windows of Number 10, as some small protest at what had happened to their comrades. Yet again, a new act of militancy came directly from women (almost invariably either Mary Leigh or Emily Davison) who wanted to protest at particularly appalling and barbaric treatment of comrades while the leadership did nothing beyond expressing the usual platitudes.

However, stone-throwing was an action against *property* and not persons – in spite of the way such incidents were described in court by police officers and reported in the press. And usually the stones were wrapped in paper carrying a wspu message. Con Lytton, for example, describes how she took great care to throw stones as low as possible against official cars to ensure there was no possibility of anyone being hurt by them (Lytton, 1914, pp. 208–12). The firing of pillar-boxes and the later firing or bombing of empty buildings were also not designed to harm people. Of course, it might be objected that burning letters was indirectly harmful. Emily Davison, the initiator of this particular militant act, tried to ensure that it wasn't, or that it would hurt only the kind of well-off people who could easily absorb consequent financial losses. This and the secret arson and bombing campaigns will be returned to later.

The NUWSS grew greatly in the period after 1906, as a direct consequence of the WSPU making feminism visible and attractive. In 1906 when the WSPU started in earnest, the NUWSS had 31 branches; in 1909, it had 130; in 1910, the start of 'violent' militancy with stone-throwing, 210; in 1914, 496. Of course, branches can be largely empty; however, membership figures show an increase from 13,161 members in 1909 to 54,592 in 1914. It is not so easy to make claims one way or the other about WSPU membership. Andrew Rosen detects a very discernible decline in membership, but quite how he does so, given that there wasn't a uniformly applied membership in the way there was in the NUWSS, is unclear. Moreover, a reduction in the WSPU formal membership or subscriptions to *The Suffragette* does not necessarily mean the same women joined the NUWSS (the new members, or a large contingent of them, could have come from elsewhere). Even if it did, they did not necessarily leave the WSPU at a local level. Indeed, there is no convincing evidence of any complete local divide between NUWSS, WFL and WSPU women at any stage. In spite of formal pronouncements by leaders, many women from different organisations supported a wide range of militant activity and worked closely together at a local level over various issues. Evidence about the Portsmouth and Newcastle areas (investigated by myself and David Neville, a Northumberland historian, respectively) shows that this was the rule, not the exception. It is a mistake to conflate formal pronouncements at the national level with the actual practices of people in the local areas in which they lived and were active. And it perhaps needs to be emphasised that at no stage did membership of the WSPU require 'active militancy'. Many issues of *The Suffragette* emphasised that there were many ways of supporting the cause – even during the period of arson attacks. The WSPU career of Edith Morrison, and of tens of thousands of other women, contrasts sharply with the more usual – and stereotypical – view of the WSPU in 1913 as a dwindling band of fanatical arsonists and bombers. The truth is more ordinary, more complex, more interesting.

This raises the interesting question of just what 'the WSPU' was, which in turn throws much light on the tactics of arson and bombing in 1913 and on whether they were indeed a product of misreading the political signs.

In writing about the history of the militant movement it has become conventional to assume that 'for Pankhursts read WSPU' and then 'for WSPU read Pankhursts'. However, such an assumption is fundamentally problematic. There were good reasons for the WSPU leadership to dislike, or to fear, Emily Davison and Mary Leigh among others. Not only did they act independently, they also – whether they wanted to or not – formed a rallying point for other women dissatisfied with the leadership, who wanted to achieve something different. A similar rallying point was the Pankhurst-sanctioned 'Young Hot-Bloods' group of younger women 'prepared for danger duty' (Raeburn, 1973, p. 96). Vera Holme, Elsie Howey, Jessie Kenney, and also Grave Roe (MofL 73.83/52) seem to have been involved in this; in May 1909 Vera, Elsie and Jessie barracked a political meeting in Bristol chaired by John Redmond, Secretary for Ireland. Rather than being close friends with Emily Davison, then, it is more likely that Elsie and Vera in some sense tried to model their militancy on the stylishness and daringness of hers.

More astute commentators on the militant suffragette scene note that militancy was never something fixed that could be defined for once and all (Holton, 1980, 1987). It consisted largely of a range of actions undertaken by different women at different times and places, in response to various events. And it is also important to remember that, in spite of the Pankhurst autocracy, each WSPU group operated with a marked degree of autonomy. Militancy grew out of the important informal links and contacts that existed between feminist women and this was different in different parts of the country.

Militancy became a *reactive* phenomenon: each shift in militant tactics was a reasoned response to a yet more repressive treatment of feminist women. What is important to note here is that this produced a reactive *leadership*: it had to respond to such developments, to harness them in some way, or it would have found itself either ousted or rendered politically irrelevant within both the formal and the informal organisation.

Thus whether Christabel Pankhurst misread the political signs is not to be decided by reference to possible new government and cabinet policies on the suffrage question at all. What one thinks of her 'tactics' depends on what 'politics' is thought to be. Most writers on the history of the militant suffragette movement appear to see politics only in terms of action that influenced the state political system. But as all feminists, then as well as now, know, 'power' (which is what the term 'politics' means) is where you experience it. For many WSPU women the formal political arena had become entirely marginal to their lives. Effectively they lived within a feminist community, with its own political arenas which had much greater everyday importance for them. These arenas of power included – but were not exclusive to – the WSPU leadership; for many women the leadership undoubtedly became a complete irrelevance and they left the WSPU in one sense, although they retained an involvement in their WSPU/feminist community (which might be based on a local branch or on an interest of some kind: in the arts, as with the Suffrage Atelier, for instance). The existence of disagreeing *national* organisations was an increasing irrelevancy to their active local comradely collaboration.

The more Christabel, in Paris, gained some sense that this might be happening, by *correctly* reading various internal WSPU political signs, the more she must have been aware that the huge and effective WSPU membership, which would turn out in large numbers on public occasions or in small numbers for other kinds of action, could slip away and leave her stranded. I am convinced that it was in order to prevent this that Christabel developed the tactic of harnessing, in a leadership-controlled form, the new kind of militancy initiated by Emily Davison.

It is important to keep in mind that these events took place in Edwardian England. Much of what happened then seems so familiar in feminist terms – like the existence of a feminist community and the development of personal politics – that it's tempting to conclude that these women were just like us, thought like us, and faced similar circumstances with the same kinds of practical, intellectual and other resources – but in fancy dress. Tempting but mistaken. Perhaps *they* were like feminists now; but the social world they lived in was incalculably more rigid, more deeply uncomprehending, more hostile to anything that smacked of an 'uppity woman'.[42]

Uppity women, like the working class at home and natives in the colonies, had to be put in their proper place. These women dared more, in relative terms, then any western feminist now could do, because they thought and dared and acted in a kind of void in which they had to create 'woman' as a human being. Women now trade on their failures as much as their successes. Like in the second of Olive Schreiner's 'Three Dreams in a Desert', we tread over those who went before; without them we could not do as we do, think as we think. We owe them a very great deal indeed.

Some male reactions to militancy were supportive throughout: the work of the two most important men's organisations, and the activities of Harold Baillie-Weaver and Charles Mansell-Moullin in particular, exemplifies this. Others were vaguely approving: that women should have the vote, dammit, could be a jolly good thing – but only as long as they asked nicely, produced good public marches and bazaars and the like, took 'no' for an answer and then went quietly away. But the militant suffragettes didn't go away, didn't take 'no' for an answer, and failed to confine themselves to 'womanly' activity. They became too loudly uppity for their own or anyone else's good, too threatening to the average male ego and the state. As represssion produced increased militancy, which in turn produced grosser repression, the behaviour of the militant women became more and more incomprehensible to male officialdom. Lunacy, madness, became the terms used, not lightly any more, but rather as the key to practical ways of disposing of the worst excesses of militancy.

Emily Davison's militant career

The context within which militant women – in particular Emily Wilding Davison – worked and tried to make practical sense of events was a complex one. It was composed of measures for dealing with militant women in prison that were developed progressively; reactions of men and officialdom outside the prisons; the ploys and silences of the WSPU leadership and reactions to this; local suffrage organisations and the women involved in them; the existence of groups of young women admirers; personal reference groups of friends and comrades; the need to stay true to deeply held principles and convictions. The best way of examining some of these aspects of 'context' is to look again at the acts of militancy with which Emily Davison was associated.

These were: (1) stone-throwing in September and October 1909; (2) setting fire to pillar-boxes in December 1911; (3) 'attempting suicide' in Holloway in June 1912; (4) whipping a Baptist minister mistaken for Lloyd George in Aberdeen in November 1912; (5) the successful bombing of Lloyd George's house in February 1913 and the unsuccessful and so unreported bombing of the Coronation Chair in St Paul's Cathedral possibly during the summer of 1912; and (6) the incident at the Derby as a result of which she died in June 1913.

It has already been pointed out that Emily's stone-throwing in 1909 was done in response to Mary Leigh's imprisonment following her protest about the events of Black Friday. Similarly, her firing of pillar-boxes in late 1911, as the report in *Votes For Women* of the deposition that Emily Davison gave to the police shows, had very specific origins: the treatment of Mary Leigh in Holloway prison for two months compared with the two-week sentence given Con Lytton (*VFW*, 1 December 1911, pp. 144–8; Con Lytton's letter to *The Times*, 13 December 1911, p. 13). Emily's statement is interesting on a number of counts (*VFW*, 29 December 1911, p. 212):

> Asked if she had anything to say, the accused said 'My motive in doing this was to protest against the vindictive sentence and treatment of my comrade, Mary Leigh, when she was last charged . . . Secondly, I wish to call upon the Government to put Woman's Suffrage in the King's speech . . . As the protest was meant to be serious, I adopted a serious course. In the agitation for reform in the past the next step after window-breaking was incendiarism, in order to draw the attention of the private citizen to the fact that this question of reform is their concern as well as that of women . . . I might have done with perfect ease a great deal more damage than I did. I contented myself with doing just that amount that would make my protest decided . . . I walked on that Thursday . . . into the Aldgate district, but would not do any damage there because the people were of a poorer class . . . the reason I offered to give myself up was that I thought that the Post Office officials might have been suspected of the deed, as there was trouble in the Post Office just then.

Mrs Pankhurst's treatment of this incident in *My Own Story* (1914) is revelatory, for she completely fails to mention Emily's main motive, openly reported in the pages of *Votes For Women*, emphasises only 'to put Women's Suffrage in the King's speech', and ignores what Emily wrote in her 'Incendiarism' essay about leadership failure to do anything concrete to protest about Mary Leigh's vindictive sentence. Nor, of course, does she mention that Emily's employment by the WSPU from around March 1910 had been terminated just before this as a consequence of her failure to obey. (Emily's favourite motto, aptly, was 'rebellion to tyrants is obedience to God'.)

Emily's June 1912 act of militancy in Holloway is more usually seen as attempted suicide, and this is treated as the main 'proof' that she meant to kill herself at the 1913 Derby. For example, according to a 1986 Newcastle 'Metro' radio documentary on Emily Davison, she attempted to commit suicide three times on this occasion, and it conjectured at length whether the Derby incident was also a suicide 'for the cause' or not. Holloway 1912 and Epsom 1913 are thus seen as inextricably interconnected in explaining the causes of Emily's 'suicide'. Olive Banks uses the more subtle argument that Emily wished for a martyr's death. In her *Feminist Dictionary* (1985, p. 63) she describes the Holloway incident as

. . . the signal for the desire for martyrdom which gradually grew stronger. In June she attempted to kill herself by jumping down an iron staircase but was saved by the netting. Nevertheless, she was severely injured . . . She began to express her belief that the vote would not be won without the deliberate sacrifice of a woman's life. Finally . . . at the Derby, she ran out on the course and flung herself at the King's horse.

A number of commentators have neatly linked the two 'suicides' via some of the arguments contained in Emily Davison's posthumously published essay, 'The price of liberty' (*The Suffragette*, 5 June 1914, p. 129). However, Emily's own writing about the Holloway incident suggests that rather than any abstract 'desire for martyrdom', the origins of her action in 1912 were again practical and specific.

During her lengthy imprisonment in Holloway from January to June 1912 Emily Davison was forcibly fed over a number of months, even though she was not on hunger-strike (*VFW*, 10 May 1912, p. 500). By the time a large contingent of other suffragette prisoners arrived, she had been without support from any other suffragette prisoners and effectively tortured for some four or five months. After Mrs Pankhurst and Emmeline and Fred Pethick-Lawrence had obtained first division (political) status in Holloway, the rest of the militant prisoners exhausted 'constitutional' methods to try to obtain the same status and they hunger-struck. Emily's own description of how she decided to kill herself was written after her release in June 1912 and submitted to *The Suffragette*, but it was not published until after her death (13 June 1913, p. 577) – one wonders just how many of Emily's other essays and reports were also received but not published. This piece does not speak of martyrdom for the cause (although the brief introduction written by an unknown hand does use the phrase), but rather of the actual events that took place that Saturday in June 1912:

> . . . a regular siege took place in Holloway. On all sides one heard crowbars, blocks and wedges being used: men battering on doors with all their might. The barricading was always followed by sounds of human struggle, suppressed cries of the victims, groans, and other horrible sounds. These sounds came nearer and nearer in my direction. My turn came . . . I lay like a log for some time . . . In my mind was the thought that some desperate protest must be made to put a stop to the hideous torture which was now being our lot. Therefore, as soon as I got out, I climbed on to the railing and threw myself out . . .

Anyone who has read a description of forcible feeding by one of the women who underwent it, such as Sylvia Pankhurst's well-known account (1931, pp. 442–7), and has any empathy or imagination at all, will reject with disgust the government's argument that forcible feeding was not dangerous and was carried out for caring reasons and in a caring spirit only. On this particular occasion many suffragette women were being forcibly fed *en masse*. For Emily, who had experienced the full horror of it over and over during her five months' imprisonment, the sound of so many voices raised in horror and terror and anguish must have been unbearable.

No wonder she wanted to do something to stop it, wanted all those other women to have a respite from what she had been suffering. But this hardly counts as 'suicide' in the contemporary sense. In a letter published in the *Pall Mall Gazette* of 19 September 1912 (press cutting in the Emily Wilding Davison papers) Emily certainly used the word to describe what she had tried to do, but we need to remember that she did so in a period before the *ideological* version of 'suicide' outlined earlier became predominant. One might as well call the action of one human who is killed trying to rescue others from danger 'suicide' ('during the sinking of the Titanic Bert Smith committed suicide rescuing three people from drowning . . .').

It is still difficult to disentangle what actually took place when the Baptist minister was whipped. Unfortunately, neither of us have been able to go to Aberdeen to consult the contemporary local newspapers so as to examine Emily's own statement made in the Aberdeen Police Court. The picture that emerges from the national and suffragette press is not a clear one.

Lloyd George was due to speak in Aberdeen at a Music Hall on the night of 30 November 1912. Three suffragettes were arrested, suspected of planting explosives; in fact these later turned out to be 'cracker corks' – the Edwardian equivalent of caps for toy guns (*Manchester Guardian*, 30 November 1912, p. 11). In a separate incident at Aberdeen railway station, 'Mary Brown', alias Emily Davison, was arrested for assaulting the Revd Forbes Jackson with a dog whip. However, a report in *The Times*, reprinted in *The Suffragette* (6 December 1912, p. 117) notes that 'The defendant denied the incident and disputed the jurisdiction of the court'. This was the only time in her militant career that Emily Davison denied any of the charges made against her, so the denial carries great weight. There are other things which add to the mystery.

The *Guardian* reported that a dog whip was found in the Music Hall when the arrests were made there.[43] When Emily cross-examined Forbes Jackson in court, he admitted that someone had offered him an apology on her behalf (which he had refused). After all the witnesses had been heard Emily said that she had made a mistake in thinking he was Lloyd George (*VFW*, 13 December 1912, p. 171). In addition, Mary Brown was Mary Leigh's name before her marriage, to which she reverted in 1914, and which was apparently an alias she had used during WSPU days as well.

So did Emily Davison dog-whip someone she thought was Lloyd George? Or did another suffragette do so while Emily was arrested for it? Or was the dog whip a 'plant' and the incident an exaggeration? Had Mary Leigh secretly left Dublin to be among the many WSPU women to demonstrate against Lloyd George? Until we see Emily's own detailed statement we aren't willing to hazard an answer. Although it is certainly possible that she did do just what the police and Forbes Jackson said, our feeling is that it is unlikely. This would have been the only incident in her militant career in which she deliberately chose to hurt another living being. It seems so out of character.

Emily Davison's known style of militancy was to do something militant and then give herself up to the authorities: the punishment given to her 'rebellion to tyrants' was part and parcel of demonstrating that tyranny existed and that rebellion was morally sanctioned. The Aberdeen incident is one possible exception to this. It has been claimed that her militancy took another new turn after she finished her sentence for this incident: on two occasions she is said to have been involved in secret bombing parties.

The successful bombing of Lloyd George's half-built house in Walton Heath in February 1913 has been definitely and publicly ascribed to her: by Sylvia Pankhurst (1931, p. 435), and by David Mitchell (1977, p. 216) in an unreferenced statement but presumably using Sylvia as his source. Where Sylvia got this information from she does not say.

Fionnula McHugh ascribes the second secret bombing to Emily in an outline (undated) produced for but not used by the BBC. She suggests that Emily planted a bomb which did not go off in Westminster Abbey in summer 1912. However, the evidence for this is circumstantial. In a letter of 18 March 1930 (MofL 57.116/76) Edith Mansell-Moullin, who was planning her memoir of Emily, asks Edith How-Martyn whether she should '(as I do) . . . leave out the bombs? Although one did actually blow a piece off the Coronation Chair!!' Fionnula McHugh concludes that Edith Mansell-Moullin is confusing an abortive attempt by Emily in 1912 with the 1914 incident in which actual bomb damage *was* done to the chair. However, the meaning of the whole letter is not entirely clear. It could be just as Fionnula McHugh has concluded. It could equally well be that Edith believed a rumour about Emily (and these were legion) or that by 1930 she had simply forgotten what happened before and what after June 1913.

In relation to both bombing incidents, we are both as yet unconvinced, on two grounds. The first is that by early 1913 Emily was so much out of favour with the leadership that she was unlikely to have been asked to participate in such ventures. The second is that Emily's style of militancy on all other known occasions, including the Derby itself, was to act publicly and give herself up. Secret bombings were more in the style of Christabel's known secret arsonists, such as Mary Richardson and Kitty Marion, and of the erstwhile 'Young Hot-Bloods'. And it's worth noting two points here. One is that even when they fired buildings wspu arsonists took immense amounts of care to ensure that no person or animal was ever physically harmed by what they did. The other is that Lilian Lenton, noted for her own acts of militant daring, was quite certain that it was various groups of *men* who were interested in and responsible for the bombings she knew about (MofL 61.218/2). We may be wrong and continue to look for more evidence on this point.

The last form of militancy engaged in by Emily Davison was the incident at the June 1913 Derby. Some commentators have interpreted this as a continuation of the unsuccessful 'martyrdom by suicide' in Holloway just over a year earlier; others have seen what happened as an impulsive dashing into the mêlée of horses: it is supposed this could only have resulted in serious injury or death and thus must have been intended as such. We think the most plausible explanation of Emily's death was that she deliberately undertook a militant act with the full knowledge that it might have fatal results. However, we do not feel it was quite the martyrdom for the cause that many people have seen it as.

The notion of Emily's suicidal martyrdom derives from two sources, both provided by her. The first is the sober, descriptive, calm statement about her attempt to kill herself in Holloway.[44] The second is the language and sentiments of her essay 'The price of liberty', in which she sets out her argument about the winning of liberty by women. She states that the true suffragette epitomises the determination of women to possess their own souls, which is necessary because men throughout history, partly through the Christian Church, have suppressed women. She then uses the parable form to compare women's liberty to the winning of a pearl of great price, in which 'the perfect Amazon is she who will sacrifice all even unto this last, to win the Pearl of Freedom for her sex'. Friendship, the good report of others, and blood ties will all be surrendered by this 'perfect Amazon'. This is following by the final three paragraphs, which Andrew Rosen (1974, pp. 199–200) has interpreted as using not religious language but sexual imagery: 'writhing', 'surrender', 'consummation' all take his eye and lead inexorably to a phallic view of her 'subconscious' association of death and sexuality.

Maybe; though I do worry about people who see sex and phallic imagery everywhere. However, a comparison with the writings of many of Emily Davison's spiritually inclined contemporaries suggests that she used this kind up 'uplifting' language because it was the only idiom available to her to express dedication, fervour and passion. Yes, certainly passion: but not all passion is sexual, for the sexual is but one version of being in a sense possessed, taken over. Many people who devote themselves to politics tend to speak if not write in such embarrassingly overblown phrases. In Emily's day feminists and socialists excelled in the judicious political use of grand, stirring and more often than not religious phrases and imagery. After all, why should God have all the best tunes? I have chosen to use one such biblical phrase in the dedication at the front of the book, for, in the right mood, intoning it sends shivers of pure delight down the spine.

But what is this essay on liberty about? Is it a manifesto for Emily Davison's own 'supreme consummation of sacrifice' enacted at the 1913 Derby? I don't think so. And nor do I think that the earlier essay describing the events in Holloway indicates anything about Emily as a 'suicidal personality' or any supposed 'desire for martyrdom which gradually grew stronger'. Again, turning attention towards the events and persons in Emily Davison's life provides the key to a less psychologically reductionist and more appropriate view of the events of June 1913.

The major event that was occurring in the militant struggle at this time was the treatment of Mrs Pankhurst. Mrs Pankhurst was continually in and out of prison under licence through the months of 1913. When in a cynical frame of mind, I wonder how much this was pure dedication to the cause – a concentrated 'do or die' attitude – and how much it was a desire to maintain control by retaining the kind of admiration that the absent Christabel had forfeited. There can be no doubt that Mrs Pankhurst was in her own way an incredibly brave and admirable woman. She had a fixed and constant goal and refused to contemplate its non-achievement. She hadn't upped and run when the militancy got tough. And by 1913 she had at least in part learned the lesson *The Freewoman* had preached: leaders should lead, not sit in comfort while followers suffered. She no longer incited people to do what she wasn't willing to take responsibility for herself. The consequence was her repeated arrest and trial, and her hunger- and thirst-strikes in prison. Consider the chronology of events.

In February 1913 Mrs Pankhurst encouraged even greater

militancy and said she would accept full responsibility for whatever ensued. The Cat and Mouse Act (the Prisoners' Temporary Discharge Act) was passed on 25 March 1913. On 3 April Mrs Pankhurst was sentenced to three years' imprisonment, there was a massive outbreak of arson and on 9 April Annie Kenney was arrested. After hunger-striking, Mrs Pankhurst was released on licence on 12 April; on 26 May she was re-arrested, and released on 30 May on licence after another hunger-strike. Many people, not just suffragettes by any means, expected all this to culminate in Mrs Pankhurst's death. After all, repeated hunger- and thirst-strikes are none too good for anyone's constitution, let alone someone in their mid-fifties.

When Emily wrote of the 'perfect Amazon . . . who will sacrifice all even unto this last' I believe she wasn't referring to herself but to Mrs Pankhurst, who was probably about to die for the cause, about to give her all without counting the cost. Emily had an enormous and long-standing admiration for such women and such giving, and she had a long history of acting in such circumstances to take upon her own shoulders the cross other women were bearing. So on 4 June 1913 she prepared to carry out a militant act that would in effect 'present a petition to the King', the petition that the WSPU had never been allowed to present.[45] Five pieces of evidence support this view.

First, just after Emily Davison's death, Rebecca West – never a starry-eyed romantic – wrote an extremely powerful and moving tribute to Emily in the *Clarion* (reprinted in West, 1982), which locates Emily's death in the context of the probable death of Mrs Pankhurst. 'They are killing Mrs Pankhurst,' she says, and expresses her anger towards a state/society that can continue to occasion the deaths of such women.

Second, among feminist groups in the North-East at this time *the* major topic of concern was the possible death of Mrs Pankhurst.[46] As this has been found locally, so we have found it among the WSPU militants who moved around the country at leadership bequest too.

Third, throughout this period, coverage of Mrs Pankhurst's series of arrests explicitly compares her persecution to the persecution of Christ, Christ the willing sacrifice. As early as 14 March 1913 the article 'Death is a Big Word' in *The Suffragette* (p. 347) reports conjectures in the press abroad that Mrs Pankhurst was going to be allowed to die on her sixth imprisonment. By 5 June 1914 (when she was still being released then re-arrested) a protest by suffragettes in St Paul's consisted of a chant, 'Oh Lord God, save Emmeline Pankhurst and all women suffering for conscience sake', and was reported under the headline 'Christ is being crucified in Holloway' (*VFW*, 5 June 1914, p. 128).

Fourth, Mary Richardson's most famous militant act, the slashing of the Rokeby Venus painting in March 1914 (*The Suffragette*, 13 March 1914, p. 491; 20 March 1914, p. 514), was also carried out as a protest against the actions of the government in relation to Mrs Pankhurst. In court she emphasised that 'they are killing Mrs Pankhurst' and that her action was undertaken to make that fact clear to the public.

Finally, there is the evidence provided by various of Emily Davison's belongings found on her. There was a race card marked with her fancies (do suicides mark race cards and place bets thirty minutes before they die?). There was also her helper's pass for the WSPU festival in Kensington that day – the card was not valid until 2.30, while the Derby itself started at 3 p.m. More circumstantially, Emily's will had been made four years before, in Manchester on 30 October 1909, just after the first forcible feedings and on a day she knew she was going to be arrested and almost certainly forcibly fed herself.

It is possible – I think probable – that by the morning of the Derby, when she collected two flags from WSPU headquarters and refused to say what they were for ('Look in the newspapers tonight,' she said), Emily Davison was planning a very public 'petition to the King' indeed, one whose motive she would be able to state in court if she was able, one that her comrades if not others would know about if she wasn't. The motive was to protest at the treatment of WSPU prisoners under the Cat and Mouse Act, and the treatment of Mrs Pankhurst in particular. It was to be effected by her stopping the King's horse Anmer, and either attaching the WSPU flags to it before she was arrested or having them found on her person if not. At least two people living in Longhorsley are convinced that this was so, for both were told by people who had witnessed it that some time earlier Emily had been spotted at a nearby horse-exercising track and was seen to grab at the bridle of a passing horse.[47]

Many commentators have said that she couldn't have hoped to stop Anmer, that the horses were coming round Tattenham corner so fast and so bunched that all she would have seen was a hurtling mass. Published photographs of what happened as she came out from under the safety rail appear to support this view: a confused bunch of horses is coming towards the viewer and then Emily Davison is tangled among them. However, we have a copy of a set of stills from a film taken by the Gaumont Picture Corporation which show something quite different, something quite conclusive.

This film was taken from a different position, almost at right-angles to the horses as they gallop past, and in the stills there is a small bunch in front, then the King's horse Anmer, then another larger bunch; there is Emily Davison, clearly waiting for this particular horse; then she has a hand on his bridle and is swinging round in front of him; and then she is caught in a terrible confusion of flying hooves, skirt and hat. Since seeing the stills we have slowed down and watched, frame by frame, a film of the Derby. It shows exactly what I have just described.

Of course this proves neither that it was 'for Mrs Pankhurst' nor 'for martyrdom', although it is pleasing to be able to conclusively nail one myth concerning her action. But it does prove that it was for a specific purpose: she *did* intend to 'take a petition to the King'. Equally, Emily Davison must have known how dangerous it would be to step out on that race course, albeit in front of just one horse, for she was neither a stupid nor a silly woman. I think she knew she might be injured or killed, hoped she would not be, but willingly took the risk. Emily was a brave and intelligent woman, a woman who was always willing to take risks when she thought the occasion required it, and who, if she was going to do it, would have carried out a dummy run to see if it were possible to accomplish it successfully. I think Emily Davison's sense of responsibility for others was great, so great that she felt she had to take upon herself if not the sins then the burdens of others: Mrs Pankhurst was to be martyred – so she ought to take that risk herself, seize that chance, to secure 'Victory! Victory!'

Ultimately, no proof of Emily Davison's motives is possible. She made no written statement about her intentions concerning the Derby act. ('The price of liberty' has no date and gives no indication of any actual act, not that this has stopped many people from concluding that it is a 'suicide note' or a 'martyrdom note'.) All that is possible is conjecture based on whatever evidence is available. We think we have gathered more evidence together than other people have been able to; our evidence, and how we have assembled it and conjectured from it, is here for readers to decide for themselves.

The socialist feminist

So far I have discussed one aspect of Emily Davison's ethical/political philosophy (like most other socialist and feminist radicals of her day she barely distinguished the ethical from the political). There has been only a brief mention of how her feminism and militancy were analytically and practically related to other critical social stances. This chapter therefore concludes with a discussion of two of Emily Davison's unpublished essays – 'May Day' and 'Incendiarism'; of her speech in court 'Gentlemen of the Jury'; and of material in Emily's Longhorsley notebook, which contains uncorrected drafts of letters to the press and an essay that she wrote between 26 August and 6 September 1912 (all of these items are in her papers in the Fawcett Library). I begin with the Longhorsley notebook.

A draft letter to the editor of the *Western Home Monthly* in Winnipeg, written on 29 August 1912 (concerning the visit of the Canadian prime minister to Britain), locates militancy in the context of responses of the press. Emily notes the earlier press boycott on reporting suffrage work, and the present press distortion of militant acts, such as the setting fire to theatre curtains in Dublin (this, of course, was Mary Leigh). The tactics developed by Parnell and the Irish Party in 1884 are emphasised as a lesson to be emulated: to put pressure directly on the government, not on individual MPs. The government, Emily insists, is trying to put women down by force – but although women may shrink, they will not be overcome.

She concludes by emphasising that women 'never used violence until violence had been used towards us' and that 'naturally in a struggle of violence we must necessarily suffer the worst' because the means that women are willing to use are 'only stones'. This points up what has been said earlier about the nature of WSPU 'violence': it consisted of the reactions of men, not the behaviour of women.

Emily's concern with Mary Leigh continues in a draft letter to the *Newcastle Journal* dated 5 September 1912. In this she makes an appeal 'of that which is now proceeding in Mountjoy prison', described as 'the degradation and unspeakable misery . . . of medieval barbarism'.

Her concern with explicating the rationale and purpose of militancy continues in a letter drafted to the *Newcastle Chronicle* on 9 September 1912. She addresses 'Mary', who in the last issue had bemoaned how it required courage now to support women's suffrage because of reactions to militancy. Far more courage is required by the militants, Emily retorts, explaining that the present position was not the militants' responsibility. She emphasises that to be involved in any kind of militancy at all involves an enormous sacrifice:

> The sacrifice varies according to circumstance. It may be loss of livelihood, position, wealth, friends, relatives and, not least common, loss of health or even possibly life. Are such sacrifices lightly made. In all this no mention of the personal shrinking a woman feels as a matter of certainty after being thrust into publicity.

She also argues that women have a duty to struggle. Brute force is against us, but behind us is moral force and right is on our side; consequently victory will be gained – and although a price may be exacted for this, it will be paid.

Perhaps the most interesting item in the notebook is an essay entitled 'The prison system from within'. This is a long piece about the necessity for and practicalities of prison reform. It begins by analysing the formal theory of prevention on which the prison system is based ('make it as awful as possible and people won't commit crimes; if they do, treating them badly in prison will prevent them doing it again' might sum this up). This is followed by a detailed account of the actual practices of everyday prison life and the deleterious effects of them on warders and prisoners alike. There is then a thorough explication of the kinds of reforms that are necessary.

This essay demonstrates that Emily Davison shared many of the concerns about prison life and prison reform that motivated Con Lytton.[48] However, she links prison conditions and the social characterstics of prisoners to a wide-ranging programme of social reform in a way that Con Lytton never did (at least on published paper):

... mere tinkering will not do. A tremendous change must take place ... our prisons are mainly filled with unfortunates who have never had a fair chance whether mentally morally or physically of taking a 'decent' or possible place in this age's economy ... these are mainly the derelicts the flotsam and jetsam of the tide of humanity who have been hauled helpless because of the hopeless condition under which they have been born and bred ... it is more than prison reform which is required it is a revision of the present structure of society it means a [word left missing] of the housing question, the question of mental and moral defectives, the question of morality of the [word left missing], of the white slave traffic, the abolition of sweating, the consideration of [word left missing], temperance. At the root of the prison-canker lies the great social problems which must be faced by the country today, in the solving of which the people of England would be wise to remember the old adage that 'two heads are better than one'.

This notebook demonstrates great concern with the vote and the question of whether militancy is the proper tactic to achieve it. However, it contains no support for the argument that women such as Emily were concerned with 'votes for women' as an end in itself. Rather, 'revision of the present structure of society' is required. The vote, it seems proper to conclude, was a means and not an end for Emily Davison, as it was for many other WSPU women.

The Longhorsley notebook dates from the period she spent with her mother recuperating from the effects of the Holloway incident.[49] The other two pieces of extended writing I discuss here are undated. However, the 'Incendiarism' essay was clearly produced after her trial in January 1913, for at the end of this essay is a copy of her speech to the jurymen at Assizes. Entitled 'Gentlemen of the Jury', it contains details of an interruption by the Recorder to tell her not to speak of the political basis of her motives.

'Incendiarism' contains Emily Davison's rationale for and a detailed description of the acts of arson in which she set fire to a number of pillar-boxes in December 1911. She makes it absolutely clear that her prime and immediate motivation was the failure of the leadership to act when Mary Leigh was given a vindictively long sentence earlier that month.

This essay and the draft of her speech to the jurymen emphasise that justice is not impartial and 'blind' to all, but is blind to women. In 'Gentlemen of the Jury' she argues that in the law, as elsewhere in government, men operate an oligarchy which acts in their favour and strikes against those who dare to resist. Although she states that she does not expect justice in a court of law, she also speaks of her determination to speak out, to act, to resist tyranny to the end:

> I stand here for justice, although I feel it is impossible to expect perfect justice in a court where every single official & person from the judge to the public is composed of men only[50] . . . I have been misrepresented to you here. It was an open protest . . . Now as to motive, it was purely political . . . Although technically you may find me guilty, morally I am not. The moral fault lies upon you the citizens of this country, who stand aside . . . the women, your mothers & sisters, stand side by side . . . I stand for the justice which you deny us.

'Sisterood' in the modern sense of the word comes through very clearly in these two-pieces of writing, as the basis of Emily's action and of the responses of other feminist women when she was finally arrested, remanded and then tried.[51] On all possible occasions she was supported by other women: they waved her off from the court when she was first taken to Holloway on remand; ensured she had the opportunity to speak to Mary Leigh while there; took messages out for her and were prepared to act if anything particularly untoward should happen to her while she was there (we ought not to forget that Sir Alfred de Reuzen had remanded her for observation – to see if she was the lunatic he was sure she must be); they turned up *en masse* when she appeared in court; brought her nice food to eat, and so on. Emily lived and worked in a women's community as surely – perhaps more surely – than many 'separatists' do now.

However, her own concern was not just for women, though it was mainly for women. One reason she gave herself up was that the postmen at the post office in question were on strike and she didn't want them blamed for what she had done. She ensured that she didn't set fire to pillar-boxes in poor areas – instead she walked into the City of London and the heart of Fleet Street. And she was penitent for having asked someone in the newspaper office she telephoned which pillar-box should be her next target, in case this had implicated them. 'Morality', then, came small as well as large and grand for Emily, in everyday courtesies and concerns for other people.

From the handwriting, I would hazard a guess her 'May Day' essay was written in 1911. She writes of her pleasure at being immersed in the large socialist crowd in Hyde Park on May Day, and links the struggles that directly concern women with a wider one:

> As a Militant Suffragist my time & energies have been fully occupied in pressing forward my own cause, which is a part of the great cause of the People.

After expressing her joy at the support of the people marching through the streets for the WSPU (its offices had just been raided), and her scorn for the idle bored rich hovering nervously outside Hyde Park on Park Lane, she emphasises that

> Socialism – represents the day of Liberty, Fraternity & Equality, when wars shall cease, when each man & woman shall labour & receive the fruits of their labours, when little children shall grow up in decent environments with full opportunities, when England and her sister-nations too shall be indeed 'merry'. I came away from this May Day Demonstration with a glimpse of the vision of the future: 'Behold I make all things new!'

Emily Davison's socialism was, like that of many active socialists of the day, something she came to through a deeply felt moral conviction. It might not be the last word in theoretical sophistication, but it is none the less socialism and absolutely genuine.

As well as writing this kind of general article, Emily was an active and involved member of the Workers Education Association and of the Central Labour College. In her papers there are notes she made for classes she took on the trades union legal position, on protective legislation, on the Trades Boards Act, and on the position of working women. Here she notes that the labour movement must wake up to the fact that the strength of a chain is that of its weakest link, and that this is precisely what women are in the 'economic chain'.

Many of her published letters to the press (collected in her book of press cuttings) also deal with such questions as 'wages for housework'. Emily's arguments against it point out that, seductive although it may appear, particularly for working-class women, the basic problem is marriage itself, not that women don't get paid for domestic responsibilities. Elsewhere she supports the right of the pit brow women to continue their work, and points out how self-seeking those union men who tried to prevent them were.

Latter-day commentators have been surprised by the radical and socialist tone of the 'In Memoriam' leaflet produced on Emily's death. The contemporary press was surprised at the size of the socialist and labour presence at her funeral.[52] Neither was anything other than what should be expected at the death of a woman who was deeply involved politically, not only as a feminist but also as a socialist, who supported through hard work many socialist as well as feminist causes, who used what education she had to benefit those who had none, who did her utmost to ensure that no actions of hers should harm those less well-off, who were as oppressed in one way as all women were in another.

The only account of militant suffragism that gives anything like the flavour of the mixture of feminism and socialism we have found in the activities of the WSPU in general, and of Emily Davison and her militant comrades in particular, is Elizabeth Robins' novel *The Convert*. In her excellent introduction Jane Marcus (1980, pp. xi, xiii) notes that

> The chief surprise for modern readers . . . is its realistic description of the importance of class alliances in the suffrage movement . . . All the speakers demand votes on the grounds that the women at the bottom . . . will benefit most . . . The novel also attacks the concept of charity and denounces 'ladies bountiful' because they don't help the poor change the conditions which imprison them.

I return to this complex mixture of feminism and socialism in the final chapter.

6
Feminist Friendship and Feminist Organisation

Feminism and public spectacles

One important and innovative aspect of WSPU militancy was the way it made women's lives a public spectacle. Instead of being ashamed of their serious interest in such things as the franchise, sweated trades and the sexual exploitation of girls, WSPU women 'came out' of their Edwardian closets into not such much daylight as *limelight*. WSPU women tramped the streets selling newspapers, erupted into the glare of political meetings, stormed around and sometimes into the House of Commons, marched in huge, joyful and immensely colourful processions like so many returning victorious Roman soldiers. How irksome for the 'man in the Clapham omnibus', but also how fascinatingly horrifying and what an endless topic for outraged twitterings and bellowings.

It is in terms of public spectacle that Emily Davison's funeral needs to be seen. David Mitchell clucks over it, comparing it to a 'mobster's farewell'. A mobster's farewell is exactly right, however, for it had just that mixture of devilry, public display, bravado; a show of strength and a spit in the eye. Her funeral was Emily Davison's last gift to the movement she cared so passionately about, for it provided the WSPU with an occasion for an immensely impressive public display of feminist solidarity. *The Suffragette* and other newspapers reported that all suffrage societies took part. This was true at the level of ordinary members, for many NUWSS women turned out, but at a national level the NUWSS failed to take part or even to send a wreath. Ray Strachey, then Assistant Secretary to the London Union, wrote to an inquiring member that 'we' deplored Emily Davison's action, however much it might have been done in good faith, for it alienated otherwise sympathetic people and might have harmed one of the jockeys (RS letter, 11 June 1913, Fawcett Library), So they deplored it; but even now it seems small-minded of them not to have taken part.

This particular 'mobster's farewell' was a truly amazing occasion. Parts of London were brought to a standstill by the long, winding, silent procession of thousands of women in WSPU colours, which thousands upon thousands of spectators lined the streets to watch. And on the following day, Morpeth was invaded by thousands of people who lined the streets to watch several hundred suffragettes and the hearse take nearly two hours to go the half mile from the railway station to the parish church. Emily Davison's funeral processions in London and Morpeth were essentially displays for the public, the last in the line of great suffragette shows of strength and presence, but more sober and more striking than any other. Gertrude Colmore's biography should be seen as another, more private kind of display, directed inwards towards feminists themselves. From its turns of phrase – and also from the assumptions it makes about what its readers can be expected to know – it is quite aparent that *The Life* was directly addressed to feminists.

Impressive though it was, the funeral procession would not have been enough to have stilled the doubts that many women must have had about Emily Davison's death and what it meant. Many must have seen it as suicide, as the act of an unbalanced fanatic, or of a singularly foolish women, just as many people now still tend to see it in these terms. A lot of 'explaining' needed to be done, and if it wasn't done by Emily Davison's friends and comrades then no one would do it. Hence the biography, which, of course, had to be sanctioned by Emily's mother, who seems to have provided a fair amount of the information in it. Gertrude Colmore was a friend of one of Emily Davison's closest friends; from Cambridgeshire days she must have known Grace Roe who, in June 1913, was running the WSPU office; she was a tried and trusted member of feminist organisations, a regular contributor of time, money and energy – and of stories. Gertrude Colmore was also a fairly well-known author outside feminist circles. What better choice could there have been for a biographer?

The production of *The Life* needs to be seen as part and parcel of

Emily's death and funeral – a single political act that took place in a context of sisterly solidarity, of drawing ranks in the face of outside adversity and also of 'inside' adversity, in the shape of an ill-disposed leadership. The death, funeral and biography each made a statement about what feminists were willing and able to do for each other. Taken together, they constitute an important statement about the feminism that these days is often negatively glosed as 'Votes For Women'.

We hope we have shown that it was a very different kind of feminism from the version that appears in most other accounts. The feminist 'careers' of Emily's various friends demonstrate this well. However, there is more to our different view of Edwardian feminism than this. Our exploration of 'feminism then' in search of Emily Davison and friends has fascinated us not least for what it has demonstrated about the nature of feminist organisation.

Feminist organisation: the web of friendship

What has most fascinated us about 'feminist organisation', women organising by and for themselves, is that the WSPU was both totally hierarchical at the top and completely non-hierarchical in its everyday presence in the lives of many women (and Emily Davison's militant career exemplifies this fact). Our reading of the feminist press of the day leaves us puzzled that other researchers have read what these papers contain and still seen a mere extension of the franchise as the preoccupation of what are often depicted and dismissed as nothing but 'bourgeois feminists'. Recent writing on the WSPU by feminist, and particularly radical feminist, researchers does much to correct this impression. None the less, in the major textbooks dealing with the suffragettes their activities and aims are portrayed narrowly and negatively, and this is still the dominant view of them for most people. In contrast our reading of the primary sources is that feminism, socialism and pacifism were the currents which, as one coherent political philosophy, fuelled the activities of WSPU women such as Emily Davison, Mary Leigh, Rose Lamartine Yates, Elinor Penn Gaskell, Edith Mansell-Moullin and Gertrude Colmore.

I write here 'WSPU women', but this itself is a simplification which our research shows will no longer pass muster for two reasons. First, the wspu should not be seen as a single entity; second, the supposed divisions of formal feminist organisations (the wspu, the wfl, the nuwss, the United Suffragists, the East London Federation of the Suffragettes (elf)) had little everyday relevance at the level of practical feminist political involvements.

Any large-scale organisation which exists on both a national and a local level – where local groups are active and involve large numbers of people – is complex and its activities are not easily summarised. Moreover, this is only to deal with the *formal* organisation. Cross-cutting this, at both levels, will be informal connections between people made on the basis of friendship, political analysis, social interests and emotional and sexual involvements. This is true of the wspu, but what has most often happened is that vast generalisations have been made about the wspu from the small bit that sticks up clearly above historical water: the formal pronouncements of the leadership. On this basis the wspu has been denounced as all things reactionary and fanatical, or lauded as all things radical and wonderful. Such simplicities are really not good enough.

As a single static entity 'the wspu' did not exist. Even at its outset the wspu was a shifting alliance of different interests, motivations and philosophies. How much more true this was during the period of its greatest expansion and activity. In addition, and almost never commented upon, how much *change* had followed from these activities. Women like Emily Davison and her friends, even women like Emmeline and Christabel Pankhurst, changed a good deal as a consequence of things they did and things that happened to them in the course of their involvement with feminism. From feminism, socialism and pacifism, the Pankhursts moved to the right. Many other women moved progressively to the left. As they moved they formed their own alliances and, by doing so, their own informal but none the less extremely influential informal feminist organisation.

We started our investigation with a prior interest in the 'web of friendship' (Smith-Rosenberg, 1975; Stanley, 1986) and thus with a more complex notion of organisation than many people have. Doing so has led us not only to recognise the shifting complexities of the wspu, but also to realise problems raised by treating even the leadership as unitary and unchanging.

In searching for Emily Davison and her friends we found out a good deal more than we had known before from published sources about the roles of Christabel and Mrs Pankhurst, and the reactions of WSPU members to them. In some ways what we call them is indicative of our assessment of the women themselves: with Christabel we are willing to be familiar, but Mrs Pankhurst is always Mrs Pankhurst.

Christabel was admired and indeed almost adulated by many; but as the suffragette movement progressed it changed and so did Christabel's own involvement: from a central figure she became a removed and almost mythical 'leader over the water', seen by only the very few (or, like Mary Leigh, the very pushy). By 1913 Christabel was still admired as the guiding hand, the supreme tactician, but by a smaller and very different group of women, women who were younger, more given to uncritical hero-worship, less politically perspicacious. Certainly by mid-1914 neither Elinor Penn Gaskell nor Rose Lamartine Yates could be counted as anything other than open critics from within; in 1913 Edith Mansell-Moullin had left the national WSPU; and long before then both Mary Leigh and Emily Davison were openly counted as rebels, disloyal to 'authority'. Thus WSPU women of some political stature themselves became far less willing to see Christabelian tactics as sensible or useful, far more willing to draw their distance and criticise, and entirely unwilling to 'do the decent thing' (as the WFL women had done in 1907) and leave the WSPU to Pankhurst control.

Mrs Pankhurst is another matter. Rebecca West's superb obituary essay on Mrs Pankhurst (1933/1982) calls her a 'reed of steel', which seems exactly right. She is a grander, more substantial figure altogether, and had a very important role in determining the strategies and tactics of the suffragette movement. For one thing, she was always *there*, always involved, and always willing to do herself what she asked other women to do. For another, she was such an immensely courageous woman; and she combined this with being – and being seen to be – a thinking and in her own way intellectual presence in the WSPU. Many women who doubted, who would otherwise have left the WSPU, remained for her sake and because of her example. Many of the suffragette women who in the period after 1918 wrote memoirs and autobiographies, and gave interviews, have noted the sharp differences in style of the various leaders.

Mrs Pankhurst was more *removed*, for she was always very much the gracious lady, but she was also more *there*: taking tea from a silver pot, poured into china cups on a silver tray, as she resolutely sat on the pavement outside the House of Commons waiting to nail an erstwhile supporter of the suffrage; daring wardresses to forcibly feed her, a large earthenware jug in a very resolute and doubtless very ladylike hand. And it was Mrs Pankhurst who proclaimed her 'do or die' strategy: either women would get the vote, or she would die in the attempt. It was thus Mrs Pankhurst who was the self-proclaimed martyr-in-the-making, who had the most 'extreme', the most 'fanatical' approach of anyone, Mrs Pankhurst who insisted on being held responsible for every act of militancy no matter what.

But there was much more to Mrs Pankhurst than this. She was said by many to be the most cerebral of the leadership in all her public speeches and pronouncements. Unfortunately, far too few of these were reported in full by the feminist press (though there are two now very rare Woman's Press books which contain some of her speeches); but those that appeared certainly bear out this assessment. For example, in 1910 Elizabeth Robins' second article on 'Why?' (the series later appeared as a Woman's Press publication) contains an almost verbatim report of a speech in which Mrs Pankhurst dealt in detail with the questions of sweated trades, women taking 'men's jobs' when men were on strike, and a number of other issues related to the labour question (*VFW*, 7 January 1910, p. 226). Unlike Annie Kenney's speeches there was no outpouring of emotion which hearers were unable to pin-point or describe the basis of afterwards; unlike Mrs Drummond, no loud insistences on home-spun wisdoms. And unlike Christabel before leaving for Paris, no concentration on the shaming nature of disenfranchisement for particular women.

This last point opens up an interesting difference in approach between Mrs Pankhurst and Christabel. For Christabel the vote was necessary to remove shame, disenfranchisement was a slight, an insult. In a 1908 lecture, 'The importance of the vote' (24 March 1908, Glasgow University Special Collection 1331, quoted in Halton, 1980, p. 30), Mrs Pankhurst emphasised that the demand for the vote encapsulated three different but overlapping meanings: it was a symbol of women's freedom; a safeguard which allowed women to protect themselves with regard to legislation; and an instrument. This is what I earlier described as seeing the vote as a 'gateway', as a means of doing something – in Emily Davison's terms, a route into being able to effect large-scale social change.

But the difference should not be made too much of. Even in the secret arson campaign Christabel never sanctioned the bombing or firing of factories or any other places of working-class employment (surely the result, not of a 'failure of tactics' as Rosen suggests, but of a deliberate and principled choice). And in their war-mongering days Christabel and Mrs Pankhurst both subscribed to a wide-reaching programme of social reform for post-war Britain which was fully outlined in *The Britannia*.

While having immense reservations about her role in the WSPU and disagreeing with her movement to parliamentary Conservatism (surely a natural progression from her WSPU role as autocrat and oligarch?), it is still very difficult not to admire Mrs Pankhurst. She was a woman who would not give up, who would not go quietly away, who knew her place – and it certainly wasn't the one men ascribed to her. Mrs Pankhurst was indeed a 'reed of steel', a dusty, unknown middle-class woman from Manchester who challenged the decidedly upper-class prime minister and government of the day, and so changed the face not only of Edwardian but consequently also of present-day formal politics. She could indeed be seen as a 'perfect Amazon', one whose likely death would call forth duty, responsibility and daring from a woman like Emily Davison.

'Martyrdom' – the assumption of responsibility and duty, the willingness to devote oneself to the cause and to give up other things for it – was a very strong current running through *all* the suffrage organisations, and indeed through other reforming social movements dating from the last quarter of the nineteenth century. When Emily Davison's 'The price of liberty' talks of feminism entailing the loss of the good report of others, of friends and of family, it offers an entirely realistic guide to its consequences. Both then and now, actually to live out one's beliefs rather than simply to mouth them in drawing rooms, common rooms, cafés and bars, is to be seen as a fanatic. Both then and now, to live out feminism is immensely threatening to other people, to the overwhelming majority of men and to many women as well.

It took great conviction and dedication to do what these courageous women did. What fuelled such conviction and dedication was the fact that, for a large number of women, feminism was the *result* (rather than as now usually the *origin*) of moral conviction and the assumption of duty. A brief glance at the militant career of Emmeline Pethick-Lawrence, a woman who was the inspiration of as many WSPU women as either of the Pankhursts, exemplifies this.

Emmeline Pethick moved from the comfortable upper middle class into an Anglican sisterhood, (see Martha Vicinus, 1985, for an excellent discussion of this), and from there into social work allied with social reform through the Esperance Girls Club. Marriage with Fred Lawrence converted him to her much more radical stance on, for example, South Africa and the Boer War; and it gave her not only access to money but also complete support in her move into a more overt feminism. In 1914 her pacifism, allied with a firm internationalism of outlook, took a militant form in her involvement in the Women's International League for Peace and Freedom (WILPF).

To many this may seem mere 'reform' rather than revolution. Elizabeth Robins' criticisms of 'ladies bountiful' may seem appropriately applied to Emmeline Pethick-Lawrence; but, as Robins herself notes in *The Convert*, there are different and more laudable kinds of middle- and upper-class involvements in social reform. The 'reformist' criticism can be no more – and no less – applied to Emmeline Pethick-Lawrence than to the many middle-class socialist and marxist feminist women active now. Neither deserve to be dismissed so cavalierly.

Emmeline Pethick-Lawrence's life was one of dedication, in which she tried her hardest to live out the principles she had evolved from her moral convictions and assessments. In this sense hers was a life of sacrifice, of giving up what she could have easily been and done for what was more difficult, what she wanted and felt she *ought* to be and to do. Ought: this is the watch-word of sacrifice; and its basis is a sense of duty, of what one expects *of oneself*. However, she is interesting to us not just because of these rather abstract qualities, but because of what their perception of them meant for many feminist women.

Both Rose Lamartine Yates and Elinor Penn Gaskell said that it was Emmeline Pethick-Lawrence's example that brought them into the feminist movement and militancy. Con Lytton (1914, pp. 9–30) said the same thing. In addition *Votes For Women* of 1 December 1911 (p. 146) records Edith Mansell-Moullin as saying in court that:

she did not try to obstruct the police, they tried to obstruct her.

She left the Caxton Hall with Mrs Pethick-Lawrence, and she was proud to say that in spite of hundreds of police she stayed with her until Mrs Pethick-Lawrence was arrested.

Even the redoubtable Mary Leigh, austere and having no truck with personality cults, was arrested and given her vindictive two-month sentence as the consequence of a series of events which had started with Emmeline Pethick-Lawrence (*VFW*, 1 December 1911, p. 145):

> The constable said . . . his jaw was still sore . . . Mrs Leigh asked him if he remembered her asking what game he thought he was playing at when he jostled Mrs Lawrence . . . asked if he could tell her what officer had her by the throat . . . She said she warned him after the first blow if he persisted hurting her she would pay him.

And pay him she did.

Of course 1911 is not 1913 or 1914; and, as I have suggested, both people and their allegiances change. In the Fawcett Library papers, as mentioned before, I came across a most intriguing WSPU visiting card dated 24 February 1913, with the signatures of Rose Lamartine Yates, Maria Tyson and Emmeline Pethick-Lawrence. In February 1913 Rose and Maria Tyson were still deeply involved in the WSPU; Emmeline and Fred had been 'banished' the previous autumn, as had Evelyn Sharp. However, she and Harold Baillie-Weaver together gave talks to WSPU branches after the 'banishment'; and this affected Harold so little that through 1913 he was at the heart of WSPU use of legal arguments to oppose attempts to close the organisation down. In addition to this, it is interesting to note that in 1914 Harold and Gertrude Colmore not only joined the committee of *Votes For Women* and stayed active in both the WSPU and the WFL, but also later that year became founding members, with the Pethick-Lawrences and Evelyn Sharp, of the United Suffragists. Later still, Gertrude and Emmeline both became involved in the British section of the WILPF, Emmeline also internationally.

It is the WILPF that has attracted most of the attention of those interested in feminist pacifism in the period after 1914. However, with some notable exceptions, the WILPF was largely composed of former NUWSS women. There was a strong pacifist current running through the WSPU from its earliest days, so what happened to these women? The first clue has already been mentioned: the two public meetings in 1915, one chaired by Rose and the other by Elinor Penn Gaskell, which protested against Pankhurst 'hijacking' of the WSPU. A second clue was found in the Emily Davison papers at the Fawcett Library: a notice which the attached card in Rose's hand points out was in the window of WSPU headquarters the day that war broke out. The notice states that the Union stands for the enfranchisement of women, for this is

> the only hope of establishing & maintaining peaceful & honourable relations between the various countries of the world. The prevention of warfare, & the cure of those evils which warfare will produce is to be found in the emancipation of the Woman half of humanity.

Rose's intention to emphasise the irony of this, given later events, and her disapproval of war-mongering, are unmistakable. Moreover, the sentiments on the WSPU notice are precisely those that underlay the WILPF.

Also in these papers is a large roll of yellowed newsprint, which is a long run of issues of *The Suffragette News Sheet*. This was a feminist publication we had not heard of before; it started in January 1916 and its history is fascinating. The statement at the head of each monthly issue is revealing:

> This News Sheet is issued by a body of members of the old WSPU who differ from their former colleagues in thinking it right to continue suffrage propaganda during the war. They have, therefore, agreed to act together under the title of *The Suffragettes of the WSPU*.

'Continuing suffrage propaganda' is not necessarily either pacifism or socialism, of course; however, much of what is contained in its pages *is*. Committee members included Mrs Emily Duval (militant mother of three equally militant daughters and of Victor Duval of the Men's Union), Gladys Evans (of Dublin days with Mary Leigh), Maria Tyson and Rose Lamartine Yates; Edith Mansell-Moullin was also involved.

However, perhaps even more interesting is the location of *The Suffragette News Sheet*: it was published from 145 High Holborn in London, the address of the WFL. So the radical rump of the WSPU,

'The Suffragettes of the WSPU', and the WFL operated from the same address. The interconnections of these two go further still: Mary Leigh started the Emily Davison Lodge, meetings of which continued at least until 1921. At a 1915 meeting of the Lodge, Mary Leigh and Sylvia Pankhurst spoke in Morpeth Market Place (*Woman's Dreadnought*, 19 June 1915, p. 268). Among those members of the Lodge who contributed to their expenses were Hertha Ayrton (who I now think must have known Emily a lot better than the tone of her 'appreciation' suggests), Elinor Penn Gaskell, Emmeline Pethick-Lawrence, Edith Mansell-Moullin and Rose Lamartine Yates. And at a 15 September meeting of the Lodge (*Woman's Dreadnought*, 25 September 1915, p. 326) donations were made by Emily's mother, Rose and also by Katherine Riddell.

So, here we have Emmeline Pethick-Lawrence in 1915 in the heart of the militant camp, among the most radical of the WSPU women, who turn out to have a deep and long-standing commitment to socialism and pacifism as central elements of their feminism. And the Lodge address? 144 High Holborn; after its move from Robert Street, Adelphi, the WFL was first at 145, but around this time it too occupied 144. The radical militant women associated with Emily Davison were at this time working cheek by jowl with the WFL. And these organisational interconnections continue, for in 1917 'The Suffragettes of the WSPU' took a large advertisement in *The Vote* (8 June 1917, p. 247) concerning a memorial meeting to be held on the anniversary of Emily Davison's death in Hyde Park; and *The Vote* was of course the WFL's newspaper.

So far a series of interconnections between the WFL, the radical rump of the WSPU, *Votes For Women*, the United Suffragists and the WILPF has been shown. There is one more fascinating link. Many of Emily Davison's friends had Independent Labour Party (ILP) connections; they also continued to work with Sylvia Pankhurst in the ELF, as the above references to the *Woman's Dreadnought* show clearly. In addition, the pages of the *Woman's Dreadnought* from 1914 to 1916 note that Gertrude Colmore gave £1 a week to its funds for a long while, then £1 a month; that Rose Lamartine Yates contributed to various of its funds (including pears to a food fund); that Evelyn Sharp, of the banished *Votes For Women* and the United Suffragists, spoke with Mary Leigh at one of its May Day gatherings (16 May 1914, p. 1); that Edith Mansell-Moullin wrote an anniversary tribute to Emily Davison for it (13 June 1914, p. 51); that Emily Duval and Mary Richardson worked for it (*Woman's Dreadnought*, 15 June 1915, p. 264). And many more of the women who were closely associated with Emily Davison are active in this period in ELF groups – as well as continuing a range of other feminist activities and diverse organisational involvements.

These widespread involvements are with the ELF in its early days; they may continue after 1916 but because of time limits we were unable to do detailed work on this. However, the links between Sylvia Pankhurst, the ELF, the *Woman's Dreadnought* and various of Emily's friends certainly did continue. In March 1921 the *Woman's Dreadnought* celebrated its seventh birthday. An article of thanks picks out George Lansbury, Mary Leigh, Edith Mansell-Moullin and a small number of others for their continued help and support over the years.

The only conclusion that can reasonably be drawn from this is that, at the level of individual feminist women and their political actions and allegiances, the organisational divisions and sharp ideological differences that most accounts of Edwardian feminism have seized upon are, at best, only a small part of the total picture. When we look at what real women did, said and believed, this picture is made immeasurably more complex, interesting and believable: these were not cardboard cut-out one-dimensional figures, but thinking and politically sophisticated women with deep and passionate convictions, clear heads, clever and ethically motivated minds.

Emily Davison, finally

And what of Emily Davison? I may seem to have come a long way from the woman herself; however, I hope to have shown that by focusing on her friendships more is revealed of the essential woman, for by uncovering her involvements we see her beliefs and principles as they were put into practice in her everyday life.

To focus on friendship, on comradship, as the mainstay not only of feminist organisation and feminist activity, but also of feminist *biography*, is something of which Emily Davison would have approved, I am certain. Emily Davison lived in a women's community – of friendship, love and support, but also of dissension and strife. She treasured all of it, the good and the bad. It motivated her, supported her, outraged her, pushed her on, provided her with ideas and a context in which to develop these and make them her own. Emily Davison was truly a 'woman-identified woman'. That didn't mean any *narrowing* of her political and moral focus; rather the reverse. Feminism was the lens through which she saw socialism, pacifism, animal rights. And, like Mary Leigh who rejected 'personalities', Emily Davison would not have understood her life in the guise in which biography is conventionally presented: the spotlight on a single individual (indeed, I would argue that *no* life can be adequately understood in this biographical format). This was a conviction they shared with many other feminists of their day. I can do no better than allow the words that Elizabeth Robins gives to Vida Levering following her conversion to feminism to make this point:

'. . . How many Shakespeares are there in all England to-day? Not one. Yet the State doesn't tumble to pieces. Railroads and ships are built, homes are kept going, and babies are born. The world goes on' – she bent over the crowd with lit eyes – 'the world goes on *by virtue of its common people*.'

There was a subdued 'Hear! hear!'

'I am not concerned that you should think we women could paint great pictures, or compose immortal music, or write good books. I am content' – and it was strange to see the pride with which she said it, a pride that might have humbled a Vere de Vere – 'I am content that we should be classed with the common people, who keep the world going. But' – her face grew softer, there was even a kind of camaraderie where before there had been shrinking – 'I'd like the world to go a good deal better . . .'

Emily Davison and her friends are, in one sense at least, not 'common people'. Most of them, like Emily and unlike the working-class Mary Leigh, were solidly middle class. Written records exist of at least some aspects of their lives and their activities, material traces of them remain, even if these have to be tracked down and supplemented by other sources, by living memory. However, in another sense these were quintessentially ordinary women, ordinary women made extraordinary by something so monstrous that they knew that it must be changed. This was – and is – women's oppression. It is this which lifts all of us out of ordinariness into the extraordinary, for 'extraordinary' is the ordinary condition of women for as long as we are seen and treated as 'not-men' and therefore as inferior.

In a sense this brings me to 'the end' – the end of this book but most certainly not of our interest in finding out more about Emily Davison and her comrades. There are many things we still want to find out, or find out more about. We are both, Ann in particular, still in pursuit of the 'missing years' of Edith Morrison between 1913 and 1952 and also of the details of her life between 1909 and 1913. Mary Leigh intrigues and interests me and I intend to find out a good deal more about her. We want to settle the question of whether Elsie Howey and Vera Holme really were close friends of Emily's. We're interested in finding out more about the Wimbledon wspu branch from its inception to the First World War. Exactly why those mainstays of the Manchester Union, Mary Gawthorpe and Dora Marsden, departed from the national wspu, and what kinds of links they retained with like-minded wspu women, is another focus of curiosity. We want to recover the details of the months that Emily spent in the Manchester area during 1909. And we want to know in what ways Emily was connected with the activities of the Newcastle wspu (a topic we had intended to explore for this book but the time factor prevented).

To find out these things will be to continue the biography which this book contains. This is because to know them will be to know more than we presently do about the complex, fascinating history of Edwardian feminism, a notable history in which Emily Davison, like other individuals, plays a minor but honourable part.

Appendices

Appendix 1: Entry by Emily Wilding Davison in the *Suffrage Annual & Woman's Who's Who* (1913)

DAVISON, MISS EMILY WILDING, B.A., Honours (London), Oxford Final Honour School in English Language and Literature (Class I.), etc. Society: W.S.P.U.; born at Blackheath; daughter of Charles Edward and Margaret Davison; joined W.S.P.U., November 1906.

Imprisonments:

(1) March 30th, 1909, one month for going on deputation;

(2) July 30th, 1909, two months for obstruction at Limehouse, released after five and a half days' hunger strike;

(3) September 4th, 1909, stone-throwing at White City, Manchester, two months, but released after two and a half days' hunger strike;

(4) October 20th, 1909, stone-throwing at Radcliffe, one month's hard labour on each count, hunger struck, forcibly fed, hosepipe incident in Strangeways prison and released at end of eight days;

(5) November 19th, 1910, broke a window inside the House of Commons; one month, hunger struck, forcibly fed, and released after eight days.

(6) December 14th, 1911, arrested for setting fire to pillar-boxes in City of Westminster; Holloway, remand one week, and

(7) January 10th, 1912 for above, sentenced at Old Bailey to six months' imprisonment; hunger struck twice with others, and twice forcibly fed; released 10 days before sentence finished on account of injuries sustained in protest made against forcible feeding;

(8) November 30th, 1912, sentenced to 10 days' imprisonment for assaulting a Baptist Minister by mistake for Mr. Lloyd-George at

Aberdeen Station; hunger struck and released at end of 4 days' fast; was arrested on great deputation together with Mrs Pankhurst, June 29th, 1909; January 19th, 1910, won case against visiting magistrates of Strangeways Prison, Manchester; has three times hidden in House of Commons – April, 1910, in hot-air shaft, April, 1911 in crypt and also in June, 1911; marches in which took part – March, 1907, July, 1910, June, 1911 and July, 1911.

Publications: Articles in 'Votes for Women' and other papers.

Recreations: swimming, cycling and studying.

Address: Longhorsley, S.O. Northumberland.

Appendix 2: Works by Gertrude Colmore

The Angel and the Outcast, Hutchinson and Co., London 1907.
A Brother of the Shadow, Noel Douglas, London, 1926.
Concerning Oliver Knox, Unwin's Novel Series, vol. 3, London, 1888.
A Conspiracy of Silence, Swan Sonnenschein and Co., London, 1889.
The Crimson Gate, Stanley Paul and Co., London, 1910.
A Daughter of Music, William Heinemann, London, 1894.
The Guardian, T. Fisher, Unwin, London, 1923.
The Guest, Edward Arnold, London, 1917.
A Ladder of Tears, A. Constable and Co., Westminster, 1904.
The Life of Emily Davison, Woman's Press, London, 1913.
A Living Epitaph, Longmans and Co., London, 1890.
Love for a Key, William Heinemann, London, 1896.
The Marble Face, Smith, Elder and Co., London, 1900.
Mr. Jones and the Governess, Women's Freedom League, London, 1913.
Poems of Love and Life, Gay and Bird, London, 1896.
Points of View, and other poems, Gay and Bird, London, 1898.
Priests of Progress, Stanley Paul and Co., London, 1908.
The Strange Story of Hester Wynne, Smith, Elder and Co., London, 1899.
Suffragette Sally, Stanley Paul and Co., London, 1911.
The Thunderbolt, T. Fisher Unwin, London, 1919.
Trades that transgress, Theosophical Order of Service, London, 1918.
A Valley of Shadows, Chatto and Windus, London, 1892.
Whispers, Hurst and Blackett, London, 1914.

Acknowledgments

In writing this book we have been helped a very great deal by a large number of people. Our debt to them can never be repaid but it can be gratefully acknowledged.

For help in the Morpeth area we would like to thank L.S. Davison, M. Davison, Alec Tweddle, Marilyn Tweddle, Miss M. Oliver, Roland Bibby, Maureen Caisley, Miss Elinor Wright and Mr and Mrs Tailor of Blackheddon Hall. For help in the Bath area we are grateful to Ted West, Mr and Mrs Brooks, Miss Claire Roberts, Angela Foreman, Florence Sloan, Mrs Alice Wickins, the Bath and Claverton Archeological Society, and Messrs Collins and Hughes. For help in the Wimbledon area our thanks are due to Miss Constance Curry, Dr Corona Trew, the General Secretary of the Theosophical Society, the General Secretary of the British Anti-Vivisection Society, and Merton Historical Society.

We would also like to thank Candida Lacey of Pandora Press for getting us interested in the first Woman's Press and Ruthie Petrie of Virago Press for suggesting we should make our look at the Woman's Press an important focus in the book. At the present-day The Women's Press we are everlastingly grateful to Ros de Lanerolle, not least for continuing the honourable tradition of its predecessor.

Three historians read an earlier draft of this book and we would like to thank them for their useful comments and reactions. Our grateful thanks to Johanna Alberti, Sheila Fletcher and David Neville, and also a reminder that we, of course, are responsible for any errors or deficiencies that remain.

We receive invaluable help and assistance from the following organisations: Manchester Records Office, Manchester Probate

Office, the National Museum of Labour History, the Civil Service Commission, the Principal Registry of the Family Division of Somerset House, the Royal Commission of Historical Manuscripts, the National Register of Archives, and the Archive of BBC Radio *Women's Hour*.

Libraries are truly wonderful institutions, often taken for granted but most certainly not by us. The librarians whose help we have enlisted have been unfailingly helpful to us, above and beyond the call of everyday duty. Nicola Johnson of the Museum of London Suffragette Collection gave us a great deal of essential help for which we are grateful. We would like to thank the registrars and archivists of the Universities of Aberdeen and Liverpool, Miss Margaret Bursdon of Morpeth Public Library, Mrs Joyce of the Bath Reference Library, and Elizabeth Heaps of the Morrell Library at the University of York. We would also like to thank Manchester Central Reference Library, Liverpool Central Library, Newcastle Central Library, Aberdeen Central Reference Library, Edinburgh Central Reference Library, Portsmouth Central Reference Library, the Library of the University of London, the Bodleian Library in Oxford, the Librarian of the Theosophical Society, the Fitzwilliam Museum in Cambridge, Cambridge Central Library, Kensington Public Library, Wimbledon Library, Lincoln's Inn Library, the Inner Temple Library, the Honourable Society of Gray's Inn, the Middle Temple Library and, last but by no means least, the Library and Information Centre of the Equal Opportunities Commission in Manchester.

The Fawcett Library is an even more wonderful institution, one unique in British feminist life. Not only in its truly invaluable contents but also in the story of its own life it holds within it a good deal of the honourable history of British feminism. The Fawcett also holds the remains of the Women's Record House collection and the surviving papers of Emily Davison. We are more grateful to the Fawcett Library – and in particular to Catherine Ireland and David Doughan, for letting us go through these in advance of cataloguing – than we can possibly express.

Liz Stanley would like to thank Sue Wise for giving house-room to yet one more dead woman. She has borne with patience living with Hannah Cullwick and her diaries for six years, then intermittent visits for months on end from Olive Schreiner, Eleanor Marx, Edith

Lees, Dora Montefiore, Constance Lytton and (still inhabiting parts of the hall) Virginia Woolf. The sudden arrival, complete with bag and baggage and several newspapers, of Emily Davison and the assembled hosts of the WSPU, the WFL and the East London Federation in the front room downstairs was taken in her stride (but I somehow think the next unexpected dead visitor might get less of a welcome). As for those furry friends Edgar and Rupert, this is the fifth book they have helped with. Edgar has left a great deal of fur in the innards of the computer and completely ripped one page to shreds in a fury of tail-chasing and roly-polying. Due to her critical commentary, the page was completely rewritten. Poor Rupert has added slow kidney failure to his long list of illnesses during the past 15 years. Hanging on to the last of his nine lives by one claw, he has also occasionally fallen into the printer and planted many feet on to the keyboard in trying to attract my attention. Any suspect sentences may therefore be put down to his inimitable help.

Liz Stanley

I would like to express my personal thanks to the following people: my special thanks go to Merna McVeigh for all her help and support through the ups and downs of writing this book. I am indebted to my friend Kathy Cotton for her hospitality up at Cullercoats where the story began; to Marion Hughes whose enthusiasm for women's history inspired me as it does all her students. Lloyd and Sandra Lee, thanks to you both for your encouragement and for keeping my motivation burning. Last but not least, special thanks to Amy Morley for being a super Mum who also took on the arduous task of looking after my three dogs Sammy, Tessy and BB Eric.

Ann Morley

References and Bibliography

Banks, Olive, *The Biographical Dictionary of British Feminists Volume One 1800–1930*, Wheatsheaf Books, Brighton, 1985.

Barrow, Margaret, *Women 1870–1928: A Guide to Printed and Archival Sources*, Mansell Publishing, London, 1981.

Bell, George, & Baillie-Weaver, Harold, *Horses in Warfare*, Humanitarian League, London, 1916.

Black, Clementina (ed), *Married Women's Work*, 1915; Ellen Mappen (ed), Virago Press, London, 1983.

Black, Naomi, 'The mothers' international: the Women's Co-operative Guild and feminist pacifism', *Women's Studies International Forum* 7, pp. 467–76, 1984.

Blackburn, Helen, *Record of Woman Suffrage*, Williams & Norgate, London, 1902.

Bussey, Gertrude, & Tims, Margaret, *Women's International League for Peace and Freedom 1915–1965*, Allen & Unwin, London, 1965.

Castle, Barbara, *Sylvia and Christabel Pankhurst*, Penguin, Harmondsworth, 1987.

Colmore, Gertrude, *Suffragette Sally/The Suffragettes*, Pandora Press, London, 1911/1986.

The Life of Emily Davison, Woman's Press, London, 1913.

Dangerfield, George, *The Strange Death of Liberal England*, McGibbon & Kay, London, 1935.

Davison, Emily, 'The price of liberty', *The Suffragette*, 5 June, p. 129, 1914.

Evans, Richard, *The Feminists*, Croom Helm, London, 1971.

Comrades and Sisters: Feminism, Socialism and Pacifism in Europe 1870–1945, Wheatsheaf Books, Brighton, 1987.

First, Ruth & Scott, Ann, *Olive Schreiner*, André Deutsch,

London, 1980.

Fisher, Kathleen, *Sun and Shadows*, Eileen Smith (ed), Stockwell, London, 1982.

Foster, Janet, & Sheppard, Julia, *British Archives: A Guide to Resources in the United Kingdom*, Macmillan, London, 1982.

Fulford, Roger, *Votes For Women*, Faber & Faber, London, 1957.

Gaffin, Jean & Thoms, David, *Caring and Sharing: The Centenary History of the Co-operative Women's Guild*, Co-operative Union Ltd, Manchester, 1983.

Gawthorpe, Mary, *Up Hill to Holloway*, Traversity Press, Maine, 1962.

Gillman, Charlotte Perkins. *Women and Economics*, Harper & Row, New York, 1898/1966.

Hamilton, Cicely, *Marriage As A Trade*, Jane Lewis (ed), The Women's Press, London, 1909/1981.

Harrison, Brain, *Separate Spheres*, Croom Helm, London, 1978.

Hearne, Dana, 'The vote and the empowerment of women: Ireland 1912–1916', Third International Interdisciplinary Congress on Women, Dublin, July 1987.

Hollis, Patricia, *Women in Public: The Women's Movement 1850–1900*, Allen & Unwin, London, 1979.

Holton, Sandra, 'Feminism and democracy: the women's suffrage movement in Britain, with particular reference to the NUWSS 1897–1918', unpublished Ph.D. thesis, University of Stirling, 1980.

Feminism and Democracy: Women's Suffrage and Reform Politics in Britain 1900–1918, Cambridge University Press, 1987.

Horowitz Murray, Janet, *Strong-Minded Women*, Penguin, Harmondsworth, 1982.

Jeffreys, Sheila, *The Spinster and her Enemies: Feminism and Sexuality 1880–1930*, Pandora Press, London, 1985.

(ed), *The Sexuality Debates*, Routledge & Kegan Paul Women's Source Library, London, 1987.

John, Angela, *By the sweat of their brow: Women Workers at Victorian Coal Mines*, Routledge & Kegan Paul, London, 1984.

Kamm, Josephine, *Rapiers and Battleaxes: The Women's Movement and its Aftermath*, Allen & Unwin, London, 1966.

Kenney, Annie, *Memoirs of a Militant*, Edward Arnold, Leeds, 1924.

Lacey, Candida (ed), *The Fawcett Library*, WSIF 10:3, 1987.

  (ed), *Barbara Smith Bodichon and the Langham Place Group*, Routledge & Kegan Paul Women's Source Library, London, 1987.

Lewis, Jane (ed), *Before the Vote was Won: Arguments For and Against Women's Suffrage 1864–1896*, Routledge & Kegan Paul Women's Source Library, London, 1987.

Liddington, Jill & Norris, Jill, *One hand tied behind us*, Virago Press, London, 1978.

Lutyens, Emily, *Candles In The Sun*, Hart-Davis, London, 1957.

Lytton, Constance, *Prisons and Prisoners*, Heinemann, London, 1914.

Mackenzie, Midge, *Shoulder To Shoulder*, Allen Lane, Harmondsworth, 1975.

McHugh, Fionnula, 'Emily Wilding Davison', unpublished paper, undated.

McPhee, Carol & Fitzgerald, Ann (eds), *The Non-Violent Militant: Selected Writings of Theresa Billington-Greig*, Routledge & Kegan Paul Women's Source Library, London, 1987.

Mappen, Ellen, *Helping Women At Work: The Women's Industrial Council 1889–1914*, Hutchinson Explorations in Feminism, London, 1985.

Marcus, Jane, 'Transatlantic Sisterhood: Labor and Suffrage Links in the Letters of Elizabeth Robins and Emmeline Pankhurst', *Signs* 3, pp. 744–55, 1978.

  (ed), *Suffrage and the Pankhursts*, Routledge & Kegan Paul Women's Source Library, London, 1988.

Markievicz, Constance, *Prison Letters of Countess Markievicz*, Esther Roper & Amanda Sebestyen (eds), Virago Press, London, 1934/1987.

Mason, Bertha, *The Story of the Women's Suffrage Movement* Sherraton & Hughes, London, 1912.

Marshall, Catherine, Ogden, C.K. & Sargant Florence, Mary, *Militarism Versus Feminism: Writings on Women and War*, Margaret Kamester & Jo Vellacott (eds), Virago Press, London, 1915/1987.

Middleton, Lucy, *Women in the Labour Movement*, Croom Helm, London, 1977.

Mitchell, David, *The Fighting Pankhursts*, Jonathan Cape, London, 1967.

Queen Christabel, Macdonald & Jane's, London, 1977.

Montefiore, Dora, *From a Victorian to a Modern*, E. Archer, London, 1927.

Morrell, Caroline, *Black Friday and Violence Against Women in the Suffragette Movement*, Women's Research and Resource Centre, London, 1981.

Morrison, E.J.D., *The History of the Parish of Claverton*, Claverton Down Women's Institute, Claverton, Somerset, 1962.

Oldfield, Sybil, *Spinsters of This Parish: The Life and Times of F.M. Mayor and Mary Sheepshanks*, Virago Press, London, 1984.

Pankhurst, Christabel, *The Great Scourge and How To End It*, Woman's Press, London, 1913.

Unshackled, Cressett Press, London, 1959.

Pankhurst, Emmeline, *Suffrage Speeches from The Dock*, Woman's Press, London, 1913.

Why We Are Militant, Woman's Press, London, 1914.

My Own Story, 1914.

Pankhurst, Richard, *Sylvia Pankhurst*, *Artist and Crusader*, Paddington Press, London, 1979.

Pankhurst, Sylvia, *The Suffragettes*, Gay & Hancock, London, 1911.

The Suffragette Movement, Virago Press, London, 1931/1977.

The Home Front, Hutchinson, London, 1932.

Peacock, Sarah, *Votes For Women: The Women's Fight in Portsmouth*, Portsmouth Papers no. 39, Portsmouth City Council, Guildhall Square, Portsmouth, 1983.

Pethick-Lawrence, Emmeline, *My Part In A Changing World*, Victor Gollancz, London, 1938.

Pethick-Lawrence, Frederick, *Fate Has Been Kind*, Hutchinson, London, 1943.

Raeburn, Antonia, *The Militant Suffragettes*, Michael Joseph, London, 1973.

Ranelson, Marian, *Petticoat Rebellion*, Lawrence & Wishart, London, 1967.

Rendall, Jane, *The Origins of Modern Feminism: Women in Britain, France and the United States, 1780–1860* Macmillan, London, 1985.

Rich, Adrienne, 'Disloyal to Civilisation', *On Lies, Secrets & Silence*, Virago Press, London pp. 275–310, 1980.

Richardson, Mary, *Laugh A Defiance*, Weidenfeld & Nicolson, London, 1953.

Roach Pierson, Ruth (ed), *Women and Peace*, Croom Helm, London, 1987.

Robertson Scott, J.W., *The Story of the Women's Institute Movement*, The Village Press, Idbury, Kingham, Oxfordshire, 1925.

Robins, Elizabeth, *The Convert*, Jane Marcus (ed), The Women's Press, London, 1907/1980.

Roll of Honour, *Suffragette Prisoners 1905–1914*, Suffragette Fellowship, London, 1955.

Romero, Patricia, *E. Sylvia Pankhurst*, Yale University Press, 1987.

Rosen, Andrew, *Rise Up, Women!* Routledge & Kegan Paul, London, 1974.

Rover, Constance, *Women's Suffrage and Party Politics 1866–1914*, Routledge & Kegan Paul, London, 1967.

Rowbotham, Sheila, *Hidden From History*, Pluto Press, London, 1974.

Sarah, Elizabeth (ed), *Reassessments of 'First Wave' Feminism*, WSIF 5.6, 1982.

Savill, Agnes, Mansell-Moulin, Charles, & Horsley, Victor, 'The forcible feeding of suffrage prisoners', *The Lancet*, 24 August 1912, pp. 549–51.

Schreiner, Olive, *Woman and Labour*, Virago Press, London, 1911.
The Story of An African Farm, Chapman & Hall, London, 1883.

Seawell, Molly Elliot, *The Ladies' Battle*, Macmillan, London, 1911.

Sharp, Evelyn, *Hertha Ayrton*, Edward Arnold, Leeds, 1924.
Unfinished Adventure, Bodley Head, London, 1933.

Smith, Dorothy, 'No one commits suicide', unpublished paper, Ontario Institute for Studies in Education, 1980.

Smith Rosenberg, Caroll, 'The female world of love and ritual: relations between women in nineteenth century America', *Signs* 1, 1975, pp. 1–29.

Smyth, Ethel, *Female Pipings in Eden*, Peter Davies, London, 1934.

Spender, Dale, *Women of ideas*, Routledge & Kegan Paul, London, 1982.
(ed), *Feminist Theorists*, The Women's Press, London, 1983.

There's Always been A Women's Movement This Century, Pandora Press, London, 1983.

(ed), *Time and Tide Wait for No Man*, Pandora Press, London, 1984.

(ed), *The Education Papers: Women's Quest for Equality in Britain 1850–1912*, Routledge & Kegan Paul Women's Source Library, London, 1987.

Stanley, Liz, 'Olive Schreiner: New Women, Free Women, All Women' in Dale Spender (ed), *Feminist Theorists*, The Women's Press, London, 1983, pp. 229–43.

(ed), *The Diaries of Hannah Cullwick*, Virago Press, London, 1984.

'*Feminism and Friendship: two essays on Olive Schreiner*', Studies in Sexual Politics no. 8, Sociology Department, University of Manchester, 1985.

'Editing Hannah Cullwick's diaries' in (ed) Feminist Research Seminar *Feminist Research Processes* Studies in Sexual Politics no. 16, Sociology Department, University of Manchester, 1987a.

'Biography as microscope or kaleidoscope? The case of 'power' in Hannah Cullwick's relationship with Arthur Munby', *WSIF*, 10.1, 1987b, pp. 19–31.

(ed), *Feminist Methodology*, Routledge & Kegan Paul, London, 1988 forthcoming.

& Wise, Sue, *Breaking Out: Feminist Consciousness and Feminist Research*, Routledge & Kegan Paul, London, 1983.

Strachey, Ray, *The Cause*, Virago Press, London, 1928/1979.

Suffrage Annual & Women's Who's Who, A.J.R. (ed), Stanley Paul & Co, London, 1913.

Swanwick, Helena, *I Have Been Young*, Victor Gollancz, London, 1935.

Taylor, Barbara, *Eve and the New Jerusalem*, Virago Press, London, 1983.

Thompson, Tierl (ed), *Dear Girl: The Diaries and Letters of Two Working Women 1897–1917*, The Women's Press, London, 1987.

Tweddle, Alec, *Town Trail for Morpethians no. 4*, Morpeth, 1985.

Vicinus, Martha, *Independent Women: Work and Community for Single Women 1850–1920*, Virago Press, London, 1985.

(ed), *Suffer And Be Still: Women in the Victorian Age*, Methuen

& Co, London, 1972.

(ed), *A Widening Sphere: Changing Roles of Victorian Women*, Methuen & Co, London, 1977.

Walkowitz, Judith, *Prostitution and Victorian Society*, Cambridge University Press, 1980.

West, Rebecca, *The Young Rebecca: Writings of Rebecca West 1911–1917*, Jane Marcus, (ed), Virago Press, London, 1982.

West, Rebecca, (1926/1984) 'The Freewoman' in Dale Spender (ed), *Time and Tide Wait for No Man*, Pandora Press, London, 1926/1984, pp. 63–68.

Willings Press Guide, British Media Publications, 1987.

Notes

1. We understand from friends who teach that this is beginning to change at least in some schools in Britain.

2. Contrary views of colonialism existed even among the colonisers. Olive Schreiner, a woman whose work particularly interests me, is an example of a white middle-class feminist critic of colonialism from within in the period dealt with in this book (First & Scott, 1980; Stanley, 1983, 1986); but of course most radical thinking on questions of ethnicity and race has come from people on the receiving end of colonialism.

3. For one discussion of this see Stanley, 1984, which is the edited Hannah Cullwick diaries, and Stanley, 1987a and 1987b, on the process of editing these diaries.

4. This book is not concerned with reassembling the 'standard biographic facts' of Emily's family history and parentage, or indeed her family relationships with siblings, cousins and so forth. Our concern has been quite specifically with Emily Davison's feminist connections. However, an important and relevant contribution to Emily Davison's biography has come from the activity of local amateur biographers. The 'By Font and Wansbeck' column in the *Morpeth Herald* during the summer of 1983 by patient research and the help of L.S. Davison assembled a complete list of Emily's half-brothers and sisters and full brothers and sisters. Her father, Charles (b. 1822, d. 1893), first married Sarah Seton Chisholm (b. 1822, d. 1866); and their children were:

Charles Chisholm, b. 1849, d. 1926
George William b. 1851, d. before 1861
Henry Jocelyn, b. 1853, d. 1914

Sarah Mary, b. 1855, d. ?
Robert Edward, b. 1856, d. ?
William Seton, b. 1858, d. ?
Amy Septima, b. 1859, d. ?
Isabella Georgiana, b. 1861, d. ?
John Anderson, b. 1864, d. ?

No wonder Sarah died young! Charles, less worn out by all this, later married Margaret Caisley (b. 1848, d. 1918) in 1868. Their children were:

Alfred Norris, b. 1868, d. 1918
Emily Wilding, b. 1872, d. 1913
Ethel Henrietta, b. 1874, d. 1880

In addition, the newsletter of the Suffragette Fellowship, *Calling All Women*, of February 1964 (MofL 73.83/59 (c)) mentions that the Emily Davison memorial meeting at the House of Commons that year was attended, among others, by Marie Stuart, Emily's niece and the daughter of 'Madame de Becker' of St Malo.

5. The Pankhurst programme of social reform which ought to follow in the wake of women's enfranchisement (see *The Britannia*, October and November 1917) demonstrates that this was a position they still held, at least publicly (and I see no convincing reason to suppose this was not their private position as well, reticence not being a strong point of either), even in the midst of their conservative and 'reactionary' phase.

6. The most impressive of such arguments is contained in Jill Liddington & Jill Norris, *One hand tied behind us* (1978). As with all good history, this account contained the seeds of its own redundancy. By enthusing and outraging in about equal measure it has occasioned much subsequent work which has fleshed out its often 'top heavy' view of feminist organisations and the divisions between them, and its passing slighting remarks about lesbianism.

7. In Britain 'national' can often be read as 'London'.

8. Throughout, we use 'the leadership' as a shorthand for the constellation of women involved in the inner leadership circle already referred to. Before autumn 1912 Emmeline Pethick-Lawrence was importantly included within it. From spring 1913 Grace Roe was included, and she continued to support the

Pankhurst leadership throughout the war, unlike the vast majority of wspu women.

9. See for example Constance Lytton's (1914) account of the extremely cordial relations between wfl and wspu prisoners and wspu acknowledgement of Charlotte Despard's importance in the militant suffragette cause in the period following the founding of the League.

10. Certainly among wfl and wspu members, there was a general support for Irish feminists working in the cause of Irish freedom (Hearne, 1987).

11. *The Times* for 22 June 1908 put attendance at the Hyde Park demonstration anywhere between 250,000 and 500,000; it was the largest mass meeting the wspu or probably any other organisation has mustered in Britain. Full reports on the prior organisation and speakers and of the meeting itself are contained in *VFW*, 18 and 25 June 1908.

12. Later these numbered some hundreds. Kensington Public Library has a collection of 79 of them, in numbered runs which go into the 300s.

13. It is customary to see Christabel Pankhurst as the leader and her mother as but a doting follower. Certainly Ethel Smyth's long and passionate involvement with Mrs Pankhurst came to an abrupt end when in a letter she suggested to Mrs Pankhurst that Christabel had gone one better than God, who had only sacrificed his son (Ethel Smyth letter to Mrs Pankhurst quoted in Mitchell, 1977, p. 350; Smyth, 1934). This may have been the *effect*, and its *origin* Christabel's removal to Paris and away from the physical and emotional nastiness of prison, hunger strikes and forced feeding. But what lay between the two was a Christabel progressively isolated and increasingly criticised, and a Mrs Pankhurst increasingly powerful, increasingly *the* dominant figure in the suffragette movement, and always insistent that her darling daughter must remain where she could direct the wspu and *The Suffragette* from safety. I tend to think that Mrs Pankhurst was having far too good a time to want Christabel back to share the daily excitement, purposefulness and admiration with her (I overstate the argument here to make a point few other commentators seem willing to consider).

14. Evelyn Sharp married Henry Nevinson after the death of his first wife, Margaret, also a feminist. A distinguished journalist, he and his colleague H.N. Brailsford resigned as leader writer for the *Daily News* over the question of forcible feeding. Nevinson was also an active member of the Men's League for Women's Suffrage.

15. As in many feminist/socialist marriages of the day, both partners took each other's names. Many of the double-barrelled 'posh' names of wspu women are in fact a product of this practice in which radical men of the day put their names where their principles were.

16. On 2 August 1914 Kitty Marion, a wspu secret arsonist, remembers being sent a telegram to cease all militancy (MofL 50.82/1124 p. 268).

17. An excited first reading of the entry for the wwsl led us to think that Gertrude Colmore had been one of its 1913 vice-presidents. Later, on a calmer re-reading we found that this had been a misreading of Mrs Baillie *Reynold*'s name.

18. In *My Own Story* (1914) Mrs Pankhurst said that the Men's League had been founded by Emmeline Pethick-Lawrence's brother-in-law. In typical Pankhurst style, his name is not given. However, from mentions picked up in *Votes For Women* over a period we conclude this must be Thomas Mortimer Budgett, who was the sole man arrested with many women following a 1909 post-Caxton Hall meeting deputation (*VFW*, 20 February 1909, p. 383).

19. See here the letter from the Revd H.K. Hope in *The Suffragette* (25 April 1913, p. 473), which provides a useful outline of the position of clergy supporters of militancy in the midst of the secret arson campaign.

20. Mary Richardson was a colleague rather than a friend of Emily Davison's (see her *Laugh A Defiance*, 1953, pp. 19–22). Interestingly, as a Christabelian secret arsonist she seems to have lived and worked almost in a vacuum. This is quite unlike the very public actions and the close comradeship and frequent meetings that existed between Emily, Mary Leigh, Charlotte Marsh and other 'freelancers'. One indication of this 'being out of it' is that Richardson is more than once quite inaccurate in simple matters of

fact – her identification of some WSPU women, for example.

21. See Con Lytton (1914, pp. 156–8) for a description of Emmeline Pethick-Lawrence telling various of Schreiner's 'dreams' to women in Holloway prison.

22. For example, Olive Banks' *Biographical Dictionary of British Feminists* (1985) contains no information about any of Emily's friends and acquaintances apart from Con Lytton and 'the leadership'. Like many discussions of feminism in the period, it deals with existing 'names' only.

23. Home Secretary McKenna had stated in the House of Commons, following stiff questioning, that on many occasions he had had suffragette prisoners examined to see if they could be certified as insane. Emily Davison herself described one such interview with doctors, following her 1912 Holloway 'suicide' action (*The Suffragette*, 13 June 1913, p. 577).

24. Her entry in the *Suffrage Annual & Women's Who's Who* notes that she founded this in 1912 after organising the Welsh contingent at the 1911 WSPU procession. It didn't disband in 1919 after partial women's suffrage was obtained, but continued to work for complete suffrage (MofL 50.70/8).

25. A recent visit by Ann found that Dorset Hall still exists, probably minus the tree that Nelson had stood under that figures in many WSPU reports of meetings there. It is now a most imposing block of flats and a listed building.

26. This was probably the basis of her admiration for Emmeline Pethick-Lawrence, whose reforming career had started in an Anglican sisterhood; with Mary Neal she had then founded the Esperance Girls Club.

27. The WSPU office had been drastically reduced and moved to smaller premises in Great Portland Street in London in August 1914. Again, this was done without any consultation.

28. A very interesting account of 'women's work' during the First World War, and of the key part played by feminists in this, is contained in Sylvia Pankhurst's *The Home Front* (1932).

29. Earlier, in the thick of the militant campaign, Lady De La Warr had been a great supporter of George Lansbury and also, financially

in particular, of the socialist newspaper the *Daily Herald*. She also gave considerable amounts to the WSPU.

30. Maria Tyson was later an active member of the Suffragette Fellowship. In 1916 she was also one of the women active in the WSPU rump who opposed Pankhurst hijacking of the WSPU to support the war.

31. At least two Riddell women were active in the Aberdeen WSPU in 1912 (see for instance *VFW*, 27 September 1912, p. 838).

32. Katherine Gillett Gatty was an active militant with a number of imprisonments and hunger strikes to her credit. She was also an active socialist (see here her 'revolution' statement in court in *VFW*, 1 December 1911, pp. 144–8).

33. In Sheffield Public Library, Local History section.

34. For a long time Ann insisted that sooner or later we would find that this woman, the 'Aberdeen friend', and Mary Leigh were one and the same. Later and with great reluctance she abandoned this theory. However, there are still mysteries here, something which doesn't quite add up in terms of the evidence we have, as the later discussion of events in Aberdeen in late 1912 shows.

35. Later a very helpful letter from a descendent of Emily's, L.S. Davison, contained the information that he too – and for reasons which I outline a little later, thought that 'Miss Morrison' and the 'loving Aberdeen friend' were one and the same.

36. Mme de Becker and, after her, her daughter Marie Stuart, placed memorial notices in *The Times* on the anniversary of Emily's death every year for around 60 years after her death. Katherine Gillett Gatty wrote of her as Emily's 'only and dearly loved sister' (KGG, 31 August 1937, Emily Davison papers, Fawcett Library); the affection was clearly reciprocated. However, as this book went to press, correspondence with a Davison family member suggested to us that Mme de Becker might in fact have been the sister of Emily's mother, not Emily herself.

37. Two women, Mary Clarke and Cecilia Haig, died as a direct – and a third, Nurse Ellen Pitfield, died as an indirect – consequence of 'Black Friday'. A fourth is Emily Davison herself.

38. Apparently Margot Asquith had the hatchet for some time as a souvenir and remembered it as being very small.

39. See here Kitty Marion's typescript memoirs in the Museum of London collection. She acted as a WSPU secret arsonist for some considerable time until the outbreak of war. Also of relevance on this point is Mary Richardson's *Laugh A Defiance* (1953).

40. Ethel Smyth (1934, p. 283) notes that the jockey, Herbert Jones, went to Mrs Pankhurst's funeral in 1928, bringing with him a wreath bearing the inscription, 'To do honour to the memory of Mrs Pankhurst and Miss Emily Davison'. As the papers had earlier noted, his wife had been a mourner in Emily's funeral procession.

41. The women concerned, too, would have been reliant for much of the time on second- or third-hand interpretations of the original events, from newspapers of all hues, but also from 'I was there and . . .' or 'I knew a woman who was there and . . .' kinds of statements.

42. The best account, accurate and detailed, of 'what it was like' for feminists in the times this book deals with is to be found in Elizabeth Robins' novel *The Convert* (1907).

43. By this time many suffragettes carried dog whips when they spoke at public meetings and the like. A letter from Helen Ogston in *Votes For Women* (10 December 1908, p. 179) points out why: as some small protection against the sexual assaults made by men on such occasions. In *The Convert* (1907) Ernestine Blunt explains the same thing to Vida Levering.

44. There is a corrected typescript of this essay in her papers in the Fawcett Library. She had sent the handwritten version to the WSPU/*Suffragette* office to be typed by the office staff there, who had returned it with a note asking her for corrections. By hand she made various changes, always in the direction of removing all mentions of police and prison officials' kindnesses, to leave the incident and the main official reactions to it stark on the page.

45. This notion of 'presenting a petition to the King' was both a symbolic and an actual wish, for time after time WSPU deputations were turned back, with varying degrees of harshness, from petitioning the King in the persons of his ministers of the crown, the

prime minister in particular. On a number of occasions Emily Davison tried to circumvent police action by avoiding the very public occasions of mass gatherings and attempting – sometimes literally – a 'backstairs' approach. In April 1910 she hid in a hot air shaft overnight in the House of Commons but was discovered before she could intrude upon an actual 'sitting' (*VFW*, 8 April 1910, p. 434). In December 1910 she broke some House of Commons' windows as a protest against the treatment of WSPU women (*VFW*, 2 December 1910, p. 152). Then in April 1911 she spent the night of the Census in a cupboard in the House of Commons (feminists tried many and varied means of avoiding being counted in the Census ennumeration); she was charged with trespass for this (*VFW*, 7 April 1911, p. 441).

46. We are indebted for this and other information about links between the various suffrage organisations active in the Newcastle area to local historian David Neville.

47. This incident may be apocryphal. However, it does sound likely that Emily, neither a stupid woman nor one 'seeking death for its own sake' (to quote the brief ungenerous comment on her death in the *Common Cause* (13 June 1913, p. 152), would practice her intended action to see if it was possible to bring off. I think she might have done just this, concluded it was possible, but misjudged the likely speed of Derby horses compared with those on a local practice track. In addition, some other almost certainly apocryphal stories can be dealt with here. Cissie Wilcox, a local WSPU woman, later claimed that she had found Emily sewing WSPU flags in secret while staying with her the night before she returned to London in June. In fact she returned to London some time before Derby Day and anyway there were a number of witnesses present when Emily got two flags from WSPU headquarters on the morning of Derby Day. There is also a story that the Derby incident was planned in Morpeth itself, and that of the WSPU women present Emily 'drew the short straw'. No other acts of WSPU militancy were decided in this way – militancy would never have happened had coercion been its basis.

48. Emily's essay was completed about a year before Con Lytton's was started. This demonstrates, not any 'cribbing', but rather that many militant suffragettes shared adherence to a similar package of 'causes'.

49. Although in fact 'recuperation' is hardly what happened. Within a few weeks of receiving very serious and permanently damaging injury, she was involved in a programme of speaking activities that would have exhausted a fully fit person – for instance, see *Votes For Women*, 27 September 1912, p. 838.

50. As women were not citizens and did not have the franchise, women could be neither law officers nor members of juries. Additionally, on this occasion as on that of many such trials, the court was entirely cleared of women. In fact Emily called Elinor Penn Gaskell as a witness, so she was able to sit in the court, the only woman there apart from Emily, for much of the proceedings.

51. 'Finally' is the operative word here: policemen refused to arrest her, passers-by ignored her action, post office officials refused to do anything to secure her arrest. In the end she had to telephone a newspaper office to inform them she was going to fire another, so that they were present and the police could not avoid arrest. The reason for all this was to deny publicity to acts of militancy.

52. The striking postmen from the depot where Emily had fired the pillar-box and given herself up sent wreaths to her funeral, clearly remembering her concern for them.

Index

The Women's Press is a feminist publishing house. We aim to publish a wide range of lively, provocative books by women, chiefly in the areas of fiction, literary and art history, physical and mental health and politics.

To receive our complete list of titles, send a large stamped addressed envelope. We can supply books direct to readers. Orders must be pre-paid in £ sterling with 60p added per title for postage and packing (70p overseas). We do, however, prefer you to support our efforts to have our books available in all bookshops.

The Women's Press, 34 Great Sutton Street, London EC1V 0DX